The MAILBOX®

Totally for TWOs

age 2

W9-BRU-417

Over **290** learning experiences for two-year-olds from the preschool edition of *The Mailbox®* magazine

- Social and emotional development
- Art and sensory explorations
- Songs, rhymes, and fingerplays
- Early language and math concepts
- Gross-motor and fine-motor development

Managing Editor: Brenda Miner

Editorial Team: Becky S. Andrews, Diane Badden, Kimberley Bruck, Karen A. Brudnak, Pam Crane, Lynette Dickerson, Sarah Foreman, Pierce Foster, Tazmen Hansen, Marsha Heim, Lori Z. Henry, Debra Liverman, Kitty Lowrance, Dorothy C. McKinney, Thad H. McLaurin, Sharon Murphy, Jennifer Nunn, Mark Rainey, Greg D. Rieves, Hope Rodgers, Eliseo De Jesus Santos II, Rebecca Saunders, Barry Slate, Sophat Theng, Rachael Traylor, Zane Williard

THE BEST OF The MAILBOX® MAGAZINE

www.themailbox.com

©2009 The Mailbox® Books
All rights reserved.
ISBN10 #1-56234-890-6 • ISBN13 #978-1-56234-890-8

Table of Contents

Anytime Experiences

Seasonal Experiences

Developmental Behaviors of Two-Year-Olds

Social and Emotional
- Imitates behavior of others
- Demonstrates increasing independence
- Shows assertiveness about preferences
- Shows awareness of own feelings and those of others
- Does assorted personal care tasks with increasing success
- Follows simple directions
- Begins to show helpfulness
- Increasingly enthusiastic about company of other children
- Begins to participate in group experiences

Language
- Understands increasingly complex spoken language
- Uses simple sentences and questions (three or more words)
- Participates in brief conversations (two or more turns)
- Enjoys books and being read to
- Pretends to read favorite books
- Shows an awareness of pictures and print
- Experiments with drawing and writing

Cognitive
- Sustains interest for increasing amounts of time
- Shows beginning understanding of cause and effect
- Understands how objects can be used
- Matches like objects
- Begins to group objects by shape and color
- Experiments with and carries out problem-solving strategies
- Engages in pretend play

Physical
- Gross Motor
  —Runs with increasing speed
  —Jumps in place
  —Kicks ball
  —Throws ball overhand using both arms (with little accuracy)
  —Catches ball with straight arms
  —Attempts to pedal and steer riding toy

- Fine Motor
  —Demonstrates increasing eye-hand coordination
  —Pours material (such as water or sand) from one container to another
  —Inserts large pegs in pegboard
  —Turns knobs and unscrews lids
  —Threads large beads
  —Begins to button large buttons
  —Begins using scissors to snip edges of paper
  —Scribbles with markers and crayons

What's Inside

Fun, Practical, and Safe Activities for Any Time...

Songs, Rhymes, and Fingerplays

I Can See

This song will familiarize children with one another's names. Use a different child's name in each verse.

(sung to the tune of "Head and Shoulders")

I can see [Susie]'s here, [Susie]'s here.
I can see [Susie]'s here, [Susie]'s here.
Since she's here, I'll touch my ear.
I can see [Susie]'s here, [Susie]'s here.

I can see [Reina]'s there, [Reina]'s there.
I can see [Reina]'s there, [Reina]'s there.
Since she's there, I'll touch my hair.
I can see [Reina]'s there, [Reina]'s there.

I can see [Sam] is in, [Sam] is in.
I can see [Sam] is in, [Sam] is in.
Since he's in, I'll touch my chin.
I can see [Sam] is in, [Sam] is in.

Early Language Skills

Pack In the Language Skills

Put on your thinking cap and get toddlers talking with this small-group activity. Show the group a container—such as a basket, a tote bag, or a small suitcase—along with items that correspond to a scenario, such as a picnic or trip. Announce a situation, such as "We're going on a picnic" or "We're going to Grandma's house." Begin by naming an item you would like to take; then place the item in the container. Invite each child, in turn, to name something she would like to pack and to tell why. Then have her place the item in the container.

Telephone a Toddler

Increase a child's verbal skills by giving him a call! For this quick activity, keep two toy phones available (or remove the cords from real phone receivers). When you'd like to have a conversation with a child, ask him to pretend that he is talking with you on the phone. Use this technique just for fun, to ask questions, or to inquire about his activity choice during free time. When the child understands the concept of phone-talking, offer to pretend to call someone he knows, such as a parent. "Dial" the number; then model talking to that person. When it is the child's turn to talk, prompt him with phrases to use, such as "How are you?" or "What are you having for lunch?"

Gross-Motor Development

Toddler Parade

Learning to balance can be tricky! So give your little ones practice by having a parade. Prepare a masking tape trail on the floor in an open area. Have your toddlers follow you in parade fashion as you walk on the trail. Or travel to the beat of a lively selection of music. Ask an adult volunteer to stop the music to cue your group to freeze. Be sure to observe and take note of how well each of your toddlers balance on the line, both while walking and standing still.

Step-by-Step

Here's another quick way to have toddlers follow your lead to improve their walking skills. With a small number of youngsters behind you, take giant steps, soft steps, stomping steps, skating steps, and more. With every small step a toddler takes, there's a giant step toward gross-motor development!

Exploring the Senses

Little Ducks

Extend the fun of the favorite song "Five Little Ducks" at your water table. Obtain a set of rubber ducks, with one large duck to represent the mother. Give each child a duck. Move the mother duck around in the water; then encourage toddlers to make their ducks follow the mother duck as you sing the song together. Quack! Quack! All your little ducks will want to come back!

Let's Go Fishing!

Put in your water table a supply of plastic fish. Place near the table a plastic pail and several fishnets. Then invite a small group of youngsters to go fishing. Encourage each visiting child to scoop up a fish with a fishnet and put it in the pail. Once all the fish have been caught, invite one of your little fishermen to release them back into the water.

...and for Every Season!

Fabulous Fall

Muddy Prints
This exploration activity is sure to interest your toddler scientists! On an autumn day, take little ones outdoors to collect twigs and leaves. Next, work with a small group of children to mix soil and water together in a shallow pan to make thick mud. Invite each child to press one of the natural objects on the mud to make an impression. Set the pan of mud and objects aside to harden for several days; then invite the group to pull off the objects to see the impressions left behind. What's next? Add water and make more mud!

Way Cool Watercolors!
Spread some autumn color with this no-mess paint palette! To prepare one, simply squirt small amounts of red, brown, orange, and yellow washable tempera paints onto a paper plate. Let the paint dry overnight. To paint, a child repeatedly wets his paintbrush in a cup of water, then brushes it across the dried paint to form a design on the plate. Younger tots may want to try fingerpainting wet fingers across the dried paints. Before you know it, your little ones will have created way cool shades of autumn color!

88 *Totally for Twos* • ©The Mailbox® Books • TEC61937

Wonderful Winter

How Do You Celebrate?
Different families have different holiday traditions. Use this simple home-to-school connection and invite parents to share their special traditions with your class. To begin, use a cassette player to record yourself describing some ways you and your family celebrate the holidays. Next, write a note to parents explaining the project and inviting them to briefly describe some of their family's holiday traditions. Send home the note, tape, and tape player with each child in turn. After each child returns the tape, play her family's holiday account for the class. When the tape is complete, play it during naptime or other quiet times to soothe your tots with familiar voices and holiday recollections.

Sweet Holiday Scents
Invite your tots to follow their noses with this idea. In advance, gather a variety of holiday treats with distinctive scents, such as a gingerbread cookie, hot chocolate mix, and a peppermint stick. Invite each child to smell the items and become familiar with the different scents. Then place each item in a separate paper bag. Hold the bag so the opening is closed almost all the way. Have a child sniff the contents of the bag without looking inside it; then ask him to identify the smell. Afterward, reward each child by allowing him to choose one of the tasty treats to sample. Hot chocolate, please!

Totally for Twos • ©The Mailbox® Books • TEC61937

Sizzling Summer

Festive Flags
Celebrate Flag Day at your art center with some creative red, white, and blue designs. Place large sheets of white paper at your easel, along with large brushes and red, white, and blue tempera paint. Encourage youngsters to paint their own designs for a patriotic classroom display.

Pop...Pop...Just Can't Stop!
Some toddlers may be frightened of the loud popping sounds made by fireworks. To prepare them to enjoy the exciting sounds, put them in charge of some popping of their own! Give each youngster a square foot of Bubble Wrap cushioning material. Tell the class that you'll count to three, and then each child may stomp on his square, popping as many of the bubbles as he can. Then let the stomping and popping begin! Have everyone stop periodically and look to see how many bubbles they've popped. Youngsters may want to try popping some bubbles with their fingers as well. Your toddlers will get so involved with the fun of popping the bubbles that they won't mind the noise a bit!

120 *Totally for Twos* • ©The Mailbox® Books • TEC61937

Spectacular Spring

Wind Races
On a really breezy day, take little ones outdoors to feel the power of nature. Give each child a leaf or a feather. Have the children toss their objects up into the air and then watch how the wind carries them along. Which one travels the farthest? Do any escape the wind? Encourage little ones to chase down their windblown treasure before returning to the classroom.

Windblown Puzzles
At this point in the year, your youngsters may be growing bored with your selection of puzzles. So try this twist to spark their interest. To prepare, assemble a puzzle on a sheet of paper (without any frame). Then spread the pieces apart a bit, to make it appear that the pieces have floated away from one another. Trace around each piece in its new position.

Give a child the tracing of the pieces and the puzzle pieces themselves (again, without any frame). Tell her that the spring wind has blown the pieces around and you need her help to reassemble the puzzle. Encourage her to match each piece to its outline. After she accomplishes this task, help her move the pieces back together to assemble the puzzle.

110 *Totally for Twos* • ©The Mailbox® Books • TEC61937

Social and Emotional Development

Picture This

This unique idea will delight your children and their families and can be used as a management tool as well. What's the tip? Use clear Con-Tact paper to attach students' family photos (or color copies of the photos) to your classroom walls. During quiet rest times, children can look at the photos. Or during a group time, lead children in moving from one family's picture to the next. Once the children are familiar with the family pictures, use them as a management tool by saying, for example, "Take the tub of blocks and sit near the picture of Ben's family."

Where, Oh Where?

Many of a toddler's emotions deal with her need for security. Try playing Peekaboo and Hide-and-Seek to help children develop a sense of security while in your care. Or play the games using items connected to their emotions, such as favorite toys and photos of parents. For example, have a child hide a picture of her mommy and then find it again. Or play Peekaboo using the photo. Where did Mommy go? Here she is!

You've Met Your Match

Looking for a fun way to help your toddlers interact? This game fosters friendships and develops matching skills. Prepare pairs of matching construction paper squares with duplicate photos of each child, as shown, so each pair of squares is a different color. Hide one square from each pair where it can be easily found and give each child one of the remaining squares. Help each youngster identify the classmate on his square; then encourage him to find his classmate's matching photo.

I'm Queen Lucy!

King and Queen of the Slide

Here's a simple way to help toddlers learn one another's names, build self-esteem, and exercise large muscles—all during outdoor play! As each boy reaches the top of the slide, have him shout, "I'm King [child's name]!" As each girl reaches the top of the slide, have her shout, "I'm Queen [child's name]!" Then have the child slide down to a loud round of applause from you and the classmates. What a powerful feeling to shout out your name! Let's slide again!

My Space

Help youngsters develop awareness of personal space with this simple rhyme. Provide each child with a carpet square or a vinyl placemat labeled with her name. Have youngsters stand on their mats as you lead them in reciting the poem shown. Repeat the activity with little ones whenever some personal space is needed!

I stretch my hands out to my sides.
I make my body big and wide.
I turn around right in my place.
This is my own special space.

Chloe

Oh, I'm Waiting

Here's a typical toddler thought: I want what I want when I want it! Waiting is easier for toddlers if they know when the delay will end. Try using a song or fingerplay to help a child who's waiting. For example, you might say, "After we sing 'The Itsy-Bitsy Spider' once, it will be your turn." Or teach your little ones this song; then encourage them to sing along when waiting is important.

(sung to the tune of "Clementine")

Oh, I'm waiting. Yes, I'm waiting.
Oh, I'm waiting for my turn.
I'll just smile and sit (stand) a while
'Cause I'm waiting for my turn.

Oh, I'm waiting for my turn....

Cleanup Categories

Once toddlers get the hang of sorting, they can really help you out at cleanup time! Demonstrate what you want the children to do by making a pile of toys from various bins or areas of your classroom. (Start with just two or three types of toys.) Then help youngsters take each toy and find its appropriate bin or shelf. Let's see... dolls in the cradle, blocks on the shelf, books in the basket. Got it!

Mine!

Yours, Mine, Ours

Is it yours, mine, or ours? Help a child distinguish what belongs to whom by gathering three sets of items: some belonging to you (book, scarf); some belonging to the child (shoes, school bag); and some belonging to the class (crayons, toys). Have the child sit with you; then enthusiastically offer him one item at a time to put away either in his cubby, in your lap, or on a class shelf. As he decides where to put each item, emphasize the words *yours, mine,* and *ours.* Also try playing this game with a small group of children to not only improve social skills but name recognition as well.

M-A-Y Day

No, it's not too early or late to celebrate M-A-Y Day—it can be any day at all! Designate each day as a M-A-Y (**Me And You**) Day for one particular child to be sure you give each child some one-on-one time. To prepare, print each child's name on an index card; then invite him to decorate the card as he wishes. Place all the cards in a special bag or box. Each morning, pull out one child's card and declare M-A-Y Day for that child. Have a one-on-one playtime with him, share a story before rest time, or invite him to sit on your lap during an activity of his choosing. This tip will help ensure every child gets a fair share of individual attention.

Weave a Web of Silent Play

Handling your emotions can be pretty exhausting. Give youngsters some quiet playtime and personal attention with this management idea. Using masking tape, make a hexagon shape on your floor with six sections that are each large enough for a child to play in with several toys. Put toys in each section; then invite a child to choose a section to sit in. Visit each section of the web so you can interact with each child.

I'm Happy and I Know It!

If a child is having a difficult time controlling his emotions, try this adaptation of a familiar song. Singing may be just the tension reliever that is needed!

(sung to the tune of "If You're Happy and You Know It")

If you're happy and you know it, show a smile.
If you're happy and you know it, show a smile.
If you're happy and you know it, you can use your face to show it.
If you're happy and you know it, show a smile.

Continue with the following:
If you're sad and you know it, make a frown.
If you're mad and you know it, make a scowl.

Playacting Puppets

Since toddlers love to pretend, try this activity to help them explore their emotions. Prepare simple puppets by drawing a happy face, a sad face, a scared face, and an angry face on each of four separate paper plates. Tape a craft stick to the back of each plate to make it a puppet. Seat two to three youngsters on the floor. In turn, ask each child to choose a puppet to lift up to her face. Talk about the facial expression; then practice making that expression on your own faces. Discuss situations that would cause that emotion. Continue until the emotion on each puppet has been explored or until interest wanes. For added fun, combine the song on this page with these puppets.

Happy Talk

Encourage students to think of things that make them happy with this simple game. Obtain a ball and invite little ones to sit in a circle with you. Begin by naming something that makes you feel happy; then roll the ball to a youngster. Ask him to tell about something that makes him feel happy; then have him roll the ball to a classmate. Continue until each child has had a turn.

Squish and Pound

If you see emotions running high in the classroom, make some slime! To make a batch, pour an amount (such as a cup or more) of cornstarch into a bowl. Slowly add warm water to the cornstarch until the mixture has a liquid consistency but is not runny. (To test for the right consistency, pinch an amount between your fingers. It will feel hard at first; then it will become runny again.) Give toddlers the slime to squish as an outlet for natural physical impulses that come with many of their emotions. It's therapeutic for your toddlers and for you.

Spinning Into Control

It's likely that you've seen a toddler's emotions change within a few moments. One minute she's happy; the next minute she's mad. Try this idea to help a young child practice getting control of her emotions. Ask a child to stand in an open space; then tell her to show you an angry face. Next explain that with a few spins, she can transform into a child with a happy face. Demonstrate this by spinning around and stopping with a smile right in front of the child. Have her practice spinning and changing her scowl into a smile. Then have her spin and change back again. One more spin and it's back to being happy. Yippee!

In Two Places at Once

Try this tip to help soothe a child who needs a minute away from the group. Record yourself singing a quiet song or reading a favorite story. Place the tape in a tape recorder in your quiet area. When a child needs a moment away from the group but you can't devote your attention to him at that time, have him sit in your quiet area and listen to the tape. This calming distraction will help give him the time he needs to collect himself.

Friendly Fellow

Keep a cuddly stuffed animal in a special place for youngsters to hold when they are feeling gloomy. If a child needs a little extra comforting, invite her to hold the friendly fellow to help lift her spirits. Don't forget to encourage her classmates to give her some tender loving care too.

Hugging Pillow

Showing affection appropriately is a wonderful attribute for toddlers to learn. Help them learn when and how with the hugging pillow. Use fabric paint to add a smiley face to a round pillow. If you notice a child hugging a friend who does not care to return the affection, offer her the hugging pillow. Explain that even though the child's playmate does not want a hug, the hugging pillow would love to receive one. While she hugs, have the child chant with you, "One, two, three. A little hug from me." Don't forget to ask for a hug for yourself!

The Sharing Song

Sharing comes straight from the heart as little ones play this game. Arrange youngsters in a circle. Give one child a heart cutout; then invite him to walk around the outside of the circle as you lead the remaining youngsters in singing the song shown. At the end of the song, have the child give the heart to a classmate; then have the two children exchange places. Repeat the activity, encouraging each child to give the heart to someone who has not had a turn. How sweet!

(sung to the tune of "London Bridge")

I am learning how to share,
How to share, how to share.
I am learning how to share.
This heart is for you.

What's Your Number?

Foster friendships in your room with this class phone book. To make one, glue a photo of each child to a large index card. Personalize each card and write a three-digit number next to the photo. Punch holes in each card; then bind the cards together with large metal rings. Place the phone book in your housekeeping area with several toy phones. Then encourage and assist youngsters as they look up their classmates' numbers to give them a ring!

Abby
314

Pretend Passengers

Use this fun suggestion to encourage children to engage in pretend play, which is an important part of social and emotional development. Arrange several chairs so they resemble seats in a car. Obtain a paper plate or similar item to use as a steering wheel. Then invite several youngsters to pretend to be your passengers. After each child is safely "fastened" in her pretend car seat, make sure to "fasten" your seat belt. Then start the car and invite little ones to choose a destination. It's amazing how far this game can go!

I'm the Teacher

Youngsters imitate a familiar social role by pretending to be an adult in charge. Invite an older toddler to wear your apron, scarf, or shoes and pretend to be you. This activity enables the child to practice imitating roles and is sure to give you insight as to what he sees as your most memorable qualities!

Let's Go Shopping!

Help little ones develop dressing skills in this makeshift clothing store. For dramatic play, gather clothes with large buttons, snaps, and zippers; shoes; hats; and other accessories appropriate for toddlers. Include a full-length mirror, a toy cash register, and paper bags. Encourage youngsters to try on different apparel and pretend to purchase their items. Your little shoppers are sure to be sold on the fun!

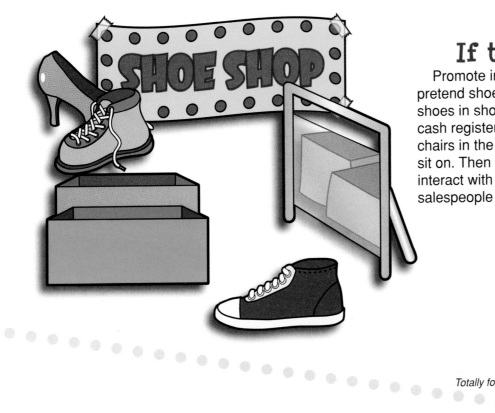

If the Shoe Fits...

Promote interactive play skills by creating a pretend shoe store. Place at a center a supply of shoes in shoeboxes, a foot-measuring tool, a toy cash register, and paper bags. Arrange several chairs in the area for your little shoe shoppers to sit on. Then guide youngsters' play to help them interact with classmates as they pretend to be salespeople and customers.

Medical Center

Try dramatic play to help ease the natural tension toddlers may feel when visiting a doctor's office. Set out a white button-up shirt to serve as a doctor's coat; a toy doctor's kit; several baby dolls; first-aid supplies, such as gauze and bandages; and paper and large crayons for writing prescriptions. Then encourage little ones to take the role of the doctor at this mock doctor's office.

Visiting the Vet

Youngsters practice caring behavior in this classroom veterinarian clinic. Gather for dramatic play several boxes to use as pet carriers or cages, a toy doctor's kit, gauze, plastic bowls for "feeding" the animals, and pet books and magazines. Invite little ones to bring stuffed animals from home to fill the clinic with patients. (Be sure to tag each toy pet with its owner's name.) Then encourage youngsters to provide the animals with lots of tender loving care.

What Should I Pack?

Toddlers explore, imitate, and pretend when they pack for imaginary excursions. To make suitcases for the trips, cover handled detergent boxes with colorful Con-Tact covering. Place the suitcases by a supply of dress-up clothes and various travel items, such as sunglasses, old cameras, binoculars, and travel brochures. Then ask little ones about their travel plans as they pack for their getaways. Bon voyage!

Row Your Boat

Little ones participate in a group activity as they help you create this makeshift boat. Cut the top or side from a large cardboard box; then cut a few portholes. Use the leftover cardboard to make a sturdy steering wheel. Then invite several youngsters at a time to help you paint the boat. Be sure to praise them for their teamwork! When the paint is dry, provide props such as a life jacket, a plastic tackle box, fishnets, and toy fish. Then encourage toddlers to set sail on the sea of imagination!

Early Language Skills

Pack In the Language Skills

Put on your thinking cap and get toddlers talking with this small-group activity. Show the group a container—such as a basket, a tote bag, or a small suitcase—along with items that correspond to a scenario, such as a picnic or trip. Announce a situation, such as "We're going on a picnic" or "We're going to Grandma's house." Begin by naming an item you would like to take; then place the item in the container. Invite each child, in turn, to name something she would like to pack and to tell why. Then have her place the item in the container.

Telephone a Toddler

Increase a child's verbal skills by giving him a call! For this quick activity, keep two toy phones available (or remove the cords from real phone receivers). When you'd like to have a conversation with a child, ask him to pretend that he is talking with you on the phone. Use this technique just for fun, to ask questions, or to inquire about his activity choice during free time. When the child understands the concept of phone-talking, offer to pretend to call someone he knows, such as a parent. "Dial" the number; then model talking to that person. When it is the child's turn to talk, prompt him with phrases to use, such as "How are you?" or "What are you having for lunch?"

Listening Wand

Toddlers demonstrate their receptive language skills with the wave of a colorful wand! Decorate a paint stick to create a wand. Gather several children together and slowly wave the wand above their heads. After a few moments, use the wand to gently tap a child's shoulder. Then ask her a simple question such as "May I have a hug?" or give a direction such as "Bring me a baby doll, please," and give her a chance to respond.

Share Bear

Help your little ones develop expressive language skills with this idea. Designate a soft, cuddly teddy bear as Share Bear. Invite three or four youngsters to join you near the bear. In turn, give each child an opportunity to hold the bear. Encourage him to share several words or a simple sentence about himself, such as what he ate for breakfast, something he likes to do with his parent, or his favorite television show.

Color Days

Try this home-school connection to help increase youngsters' vocabulary and introduce colors. Designate a different color for each day of the week. Send a note home to parents asking them to dress their child in clothing or accessories of the corresponding color for each designated color day. Then invite little ones to talk about what they are wearing, encouraging each child to name the color.

Feel and Name

Little ones name familiar objects when they play this guessing game. Display several items, such as a toy car, a baby doll, a cup, and a hairbrush. Encourage youngsters to feel and name each item; then conceal the items in a pillowcase. In turn, invite each child to reach into the pillowcase, feel an item, and then guess what it is. Have her remove the item to check her guess. Finally, have her put the item back in the pillowcase and then continue play with the next student.

Show and Tell

Use this idea to help youngsters understand that pictures have meaning. Gather several photos or magazine pictures, such as a child crying, children playing at a park, or a doctor examining a baby. Show each picture, in turn, and invite little ones to tell you what they see happening. Then encourage youngsters to talk about similar events in their lives.

How's the Weather?

With this idea, toddlers build simple environmental vocabulary and observation skills! Gather children around a window or take them outside; then sing the song shown. When the song is over, help youngsters describe the weather using simple words, such as *sunny, cloudy, rainy, cold,* and *hot.* Then encourage little ones to name clothing or accessories needed for the current weather conditions, such as a raincoat, shorts, a sweater, or sunglasses.

(sung to the tune of "Where Is Thumbkin?")

Weather watchers, weather watchers,
What do you see? What do you see?
Tell me what the weather's like.
Tell me what the weather's like.
Won't you please? Won't you please?

Landmarks for Language

Here's an idea that helps youngsters use their language skills and reinforces colors and shapes at the same time. In each area of your classroom, secure to the floor a large shape of a different color. For example, attach a blue star to the floor in your block area and a yellow star to the floor in your group area. Refer to these shapes when giving directions to your toddlers. You might say, "Sit near the yellow star for storytime" or "Wait by the red star to go outside." Change the shapes periodically to keep your little ones listening, looking, and learning!

Wake Up!

Rise and shine! This activity will help awaken youngsters' ability to listen and follow simple directions. Ask little ones to pretend they are sleepy, and have them practice stretching their bodies from their fingers to their toes. Next, have them lie down on the floor and pretend they are asleep. Explain that when you say, "It's time to wake up!" they should slowly stretch their bodies and open their eyes. When you say, "It's time to go to sleep," they should close their eyes and lie very still. Aahhhh, was that a yawn?

Directed Dancing

"Put away your toy, sit at the table, and then take a cup from the stack." Wow! That's a lot to remember when you're two! Help toddlers practice following two-step directions in a fun, musical way. As you play a recording of dance music, demonstrate a short series of movements and give the verbal directions to match, such as "Stomp and clap." Once your youngsters are able to keep up, make the directions more complex. Let the dancing and following directions begin!

Pick a Part

This simple game helps your little ones learn to identify body parts. Give each youngster a seasonal cutout. As you name a body part, encourage each child to place his cutout on that part of his body. Ready now? Put an apple on your head. Put an apple on your foot!

Name That Noise

Can you guess what this game encourages? Listening and speaking, of course. Invite your children to watch and listen as you record familiar sounds—such as a door closing and blocks falling—and then play each sound back again. When you have finished making the tape, replay it and have the children take turns naming the sounds. Very soon you'll hear the results of their increased listening skills.

Surprise Me

Playing this game improves little ones' language and memory skills. To make a guessing game, use a utility knife to cut four or more square flaps in a sheet of poster board, making sure that the flaps are spaced apart evenly. Lift each flap and fold it along the uncut side. Attach the sheet of cut poster board to a second sheet of poster board. Beneath each flap, tape a different magazine picture, clip art image, or photo to the bottom sheet of poster board. To use the game, invite a child to look under each flap and describe what he sees. Then have him close the flaps and guess what is under a flap before lifting it again. Vary the pictures by season, holiday, or theme.

Book Surprises

Try this tip to get your toddlers into books. Cut several circles from colorful construction paper, sizing them so they'll fit between the pages of a board book from your classroom collection. Tuck the circles between the pages in a few spots; then show the book to a small group of children. Encourage them to find the surprises hiding inside it. Tuck similar surprises of different colors and shapes into other books on your library shelf. Before you know it, little ones will be finding the *real* treasures hiding in books!

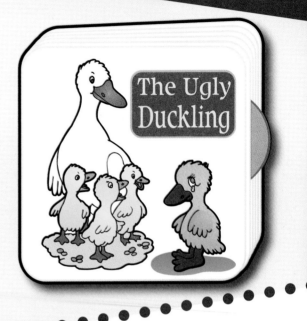

The Ugly Duckling

Quiet-Time Imagination

Even your quiet resting times can be learning times for toddlers. While youngsters rest, reread a familiar story. Instead of showing the illustrations, describe them. Softly tell your listening resters what the characters are wearing, what they are doing, and what their facial expressions look like. Your little ones will not only hear the story, but they'll imagine it too!

Early Math Skills

How Many Is a Handful?

Toddlers help count objects and explore texture with this activity. Place ten pom-poms in a gift bag. Invite a child to reach in the bag, grab a handful of pom-poms, and then place them on the floor. Count the pom-poms aloud, encouraging her to count along with you. If desired, repeat the activity using different materials, such as LEGO toy pieces, cotton balls, and large pencil erasers.

Boxful of Bows

This simple idea gives little ones plenty of practice with counting. Gather a group of youngsters around a lidless gift-wrapped box full of bows. Turn the box over so the contents spill on the floor. Then invite toddlers to count along with you as you drop each bow back in the box.

Count to Ten!

Counting to ten is lots of fun when rhythm instruments are used! Distribute a variety of instruments. Then lead youngsters in singing the song shown, instructing each child to play his instrument as he counts aloud.

If you're happy and you know it, count to ten.
1-2-3-4-5-6-7-8-9-10!   *Count aloud and play instruments.*
If you're happy and you know it, count to ten.
1-2-3-4-5-6-7-8-9-10!   *Count aloud and play instruments.*
If you're happy and you know it
And you really want to show it,
If you're happy and you know it, count to ten.
1-2-3-4-5-6-7-8-9-10!   *Count aloud and play instruments.*

Body Builders

Help little ones reach new heights with this counting idea. Encourage youngsters to build structures from the floor to various parts of their bodies. For example, you might ask a child to build a tower that reaches her knees. When she has finished building her tower, help her count aloud the number of blocks used.

One, Two—Toddlers Can Do!

I have two trucks!

Help your toddlers develop their emerging number sense with this activity that emphasizes identifying two. Collect pairs of items from around your classroom, such as two trucks, two crayons, and two paper cups. Show each pair to the children and say the chant below, substituting the appropriate description for the underlined words. Then place one item from each pair somewhere in the room. Give a remaining item to a child and ask him to find its partner. As the child joins the pair, repeat the chant and encourage the children to join in. Continue with other items until every child has had a chance to find a pair.

Two [trucks].
Two I see!
Two [trucks]
In front of me!

Soft and Touchable

Try these nifty tactile cards to help little ones count using one-to-one correspondence. Hot-glue sets of pom-poms to tagboard squares. Then invite a youngster to count the pom-poms on each card, guiding him to say one number for each pom-pom he touches.

Fine China

Toddlers practice one-to-one correspondence using a collection of dinnerware and food! Set out four or five plastic plates along with a bowl containing a matching number of plastic food items. Invite a child to help serve lunch by placing one food item on each plate. These portions are just right!

Counting on Cookies

Youngsters reinforce one-to-one correspondence skills and get a fine-motor workout with this idea! To prepare, use masking tape to divide two or three cookie sheets into six sections each. Place the cookie sheets at a table along with a batch of brown play dough. Invite a child to make one play dough cookie for each section on her tray. When she is finished, help her count the cookies aloud.

Roll and Count

Introduce toddlers to numbers with this catchy idea that reinforces counting. Write a different number on each section of an inflated beach ball. Invite youngsters to sit in a row. Roll the ball to a child and ask him to point to one of the numbers. Announce the name of the number; then count aloud as you lead little ones in performing an action, such as clapping or touching toes, the identified number of times. Then have the child roll the ball back to you.

Size It Up

Use this idea to introduce youngsters to the concepts of big and small. Obtain two plastic pails: one big and one small. Attach to each pail a corresponding-size pom-pom. Also provide a supply of pom-poms in each size. Gather a small group of youngsters and talk about the different-size pails and pom-poms. Next, invite each child, in turn, to take a pom-pom. Then ask her which pail she thinks it belongs in. After confirming her answer, have her put the pom-pom in that pail.

More or Less

Little ones get a real feel for what it means to have more or less with this whole-body activity! Place a plastic hoop on the floor and invite several youngsters to step inside. Then ask a child to tell you whether there should be more or fewer children in the hoop. If she says more, have one or two children step inside the hoop. If she says fewer, have one or two children hop out of the hoop. Continue in the same manner to create sets of more and less.

Spill and Sort

Say yes to toddlers doing their favorite activity—dumping toys!— and then help them learn to sort. Fill each of two plastic tubs with a different type of toy; then label each tub with a corresponding picture and word. Place the tubs on the floor and invite several children to help you dump the toys and mix them together. Next, point to each picture and read the word. Encourage little ones to help you put each toy back in its corresponding tub.

Tidy Kitchen

Youngsters help keep the play kitchen organized with this sorting activity. Place at your housekeeping table a plastic flatware tray and a basket of plastic forks, spoons, and knives. Place one of each utensil in a separate compartment to use as a sorting guide. Then invite two children to help you put the remaining utensils in the appropriate compartments.

Load 'em Up!

Stock your block center with large plastic dump trucks and other toy trucks just right for hauling. (Ask for toy donations from parents or search for deals at yard sales or thrift stores.) Also stock the center with lots of cargo that youngsters can load onto and unload from the trucks (such as cotton balls, jar lids, and large empty thread spools). Store each different set of items in a separate plastic container. On the lid of each container, glue a sample of the items stored inside. Encourage youngsters to use the trucks to load and unload the items. At the end of activity time, help youngsters return each item to its container. Then have them park their rigs neatly in your block center's truck yard.

Laundry Helpers

Little ones develop matching skills and friendships with the help of this laundry center! Place different-colored pairs of socks in a laundry basket. Invite two youngsters to dump the socks out of the basket. Then encourage each child to find matching pairs of socks and put them back in the basket.

Circles and Bows

Engage your little ones in this color-recognition game. In advance, place a supply of different-colored bows in a gift bag. Place a corresponding-color circle on the floor for each color of bow. Gather youngsters together; then invite each child to pick a bow from the bag. Once everyone has had a turn, ask each child to stand by the circle that matches the color of her bow.

Surprise Box

Use this fun idea to help little ones identify colors. To prepare, fill a lidded box with items of different colors. Using a confused facial expression, show the box to youngsters and tell them someone left it outside the door. Then pique toddlers' curiosity by gently shaking the box so they hear the items moving. Next, open the box with caution, and then show a look of surprise! Finally, invite each child, in turn, to choose an item from the box. Then encourage him to name the item and its color, providing help as needed.

I Spy Something Blue

All eyes are searching for something blue with this investigative idea. Provide each child with a cardboard tube that has been painted blue. Have each youngster hold his tube to his eye like a spyglass and look for blue objects around the classroom. Encourage each child to name a blue object that he spies. Then take youngsters outside to search for other blue items. I spy a blue sky!

Yellow, Yellow, Everywhere!

To prepare for this yellow hunt, secretly place yellow shape cutouts—such as bananas, stars, apples, and flowers—in the classroom where they can easily be found. Then invite each child to look around the room to find one yellow shape. During the yellow hunt, sing this bright, cheery song.

(sung to the tune of "Twinkle, Twinkle, Little Star")

Yellow, yellow, bright and fair,
Yellow, yellow, everywhere.
Lemonade and apples too;
Golden yellow hair on you.
Yellow, yellow, bright and fair,
Yellow, yellow, everywhere.

"Color-rific" Grab Bag!

Older toddlers use their thinking caps with this idea that focuses on the color red. Conceal a red item—such as a crayon, an apple, or a mitten—in a bag. Then give youngsters clues about the object and have them try to guess what it is. After the object has been guessed, reveal the item in the bag. If desired, repeat the activity using a different-colored object.

Sort-a-Snack

Your little ones will put this cereal-sorting activity in the "tasty" category! Provide a child with a clean muffin tin and a serving of fruit-flavored, O-shaped cereal. Show her how to sort one color of cereal pieces into a cup. Then encourage her to sort the rest of her cereal. Once she's sorted, it's time to eat this colorful treat!

All Sorts of Fun

Use colored tape to divide a round or square table into a sorting area with two, three, or four sections. To encourage students to sort by color, tape a different-colored shape in each section. Keep a variety of manipulatives nearby so that individual students or small groups can come to the table for plenty of sorting fun.

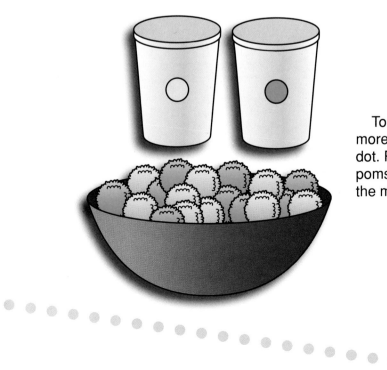

Polka-Dot Cups

To prepare for this color-sorting activity, program two or more clear plastic cups each with a different-colored sticky dot. Provide a container of large corresponding-color pom-poms. Encourage a youngster to place each pom-pom in the matching cup.

Tabletop Flannelboard

Transform an unused table into an instant flannelboard with this handy idea. Cut a piece of felt to match the dimensions of a small tabletop. Use double-sided tape to attach the piece to the tabletop. Then attach a variety of felt shapes to the table. Place nearby felt shapes that match the ones on the table. A child places a matching shape on top of each shape on the table.

Painting Takes Shape

With this idea, little ones' creative efforts really take shape. Use masking tape to make outlines of geometric shapes on large sheets of fingerpaint paper. Encourage a young artist to fingerpaint over an entire sheet of paper. When the paint is dry, assist her in carefully removing the tape. Surprise! What shapes did you paint?

Block Buildup

Math skills will really stack up with this constructive idea. Trace blocks of a variety of shapes and sizes onto pieces of construction paper. Cut out the shapes; then laminate them for durability. Tape the cutouts to the floor of your block area. Challenge youngsters to build block towers that correspond to each cutout's shape. This center is a blockbuster!

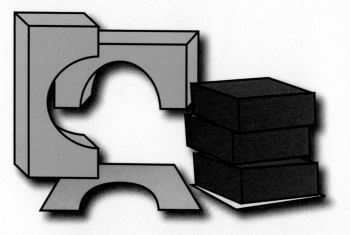

Keep It Going

Use these simple ideas to keep your little ones' understanding of math concepts afloat! Cut sponges into geometric shapes and put them in the water table or encourage pouring and filling by adding muffin tins, measuring cups, spoons, and graduated nesting cups to the water table.

It's Circle Time!

Help youngsters discover the wonderful world of circles with this idea. Use masking tape to make an oversize circle outline on the floor. Invite little ones to stand on the outline. Then get their math muscles moving with this shapely song. Create new verses by replacing the underlined words with other movements, such as *stomp your feet, slide sideways,* and *hop up and down.*

(sung to the tune of "If You're Happy and You Know It")

[Tiptoe slowly] on the circle and go round.
[Tiptoe slowly] on the circle and go round.
[Tiptoe slowly] on the circle and go round
and round and round.
[Tiptoe slowly] on the circle and go round.

Dear Parent, Go on a circle hunt! Help your child learn about circles by looking for circles at home.

Searching for Circles

Take youngsters outside for a circle search. Lead students on a circle walk around your school, keeping a list as they observe circles along the way. Include families in the fun by sending home a circular note suggesting that they conduct their own circle hunt.

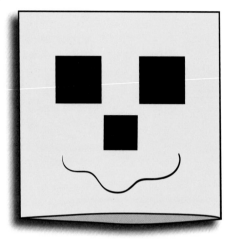

Celebrity Square

Assist each child in making a square puppet to add personality to your focus on squares. To make a puppet, cut a construction paper rectangle that measures exactly twice as long as it is wide. Fold the rectangle in half; then glue only the sides together. Encourage each child to use small paper squares and markers as desired to add facial features to his square. Teach youngsters the following song and encourage them to help their square puppets sing along!

(sung to the tune of "London Bridge")

My four sides are just the same,
Just the same, just the same.
My four sides are just the same.
I'm a square.

Triangle Town

Where's the best place to learn about triangles? Triangle Town, of course! In an open area of your room, establish the boundaries of Triangle Town by using colored tape to outline a large triangle on the floor. Randomly tape smaller triangles inside the large triangle to create a maze of roads. Provide youngsters with various colors of construction paper triangles, markers, glue, and cardboard tubes. Encourage them to create triangle trees and signs for Triangle Town. Supply triangular-shaped blocks and small cars for youngsters to play with while visiting the town.

Let's Bowl!

Youngsters will love setting up triangles in this easy-to-make game of bowling. Locate an area suitable for bowling, such as a sidewalk, a hall, or an open area of your classroom. Set up ten cardboard tubes to form a triangle. Mark around the triangular arrangement with chalk. (If the bowling lane will be indoors, use masking tape.) If desired, also mark the spot where each tube should be placed to form the bowling arrangement. To play, a child rolls a soft ball toward the set-up tubes. Encourage each child to count the tubes in the triangular arrangement when preparing for the next set.

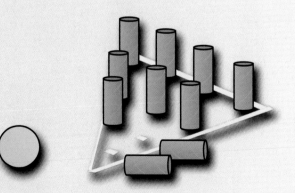

Musical Shapes

Shape up, move to the beat, and tell me what shape is under your feet! For each child, cut out a large construction paper shape, such as a circle, square, triangle, or heart. Attach the cutouts to the floor to make a large circle. Invite each child to stand on a shape; then play a recording of music. Have youngsters walk around the circle from shape to shape. Stop the music and invite a volunteer to name the shape he is standing on, providing help as needed.

Where Is Teddy?

Little ones learn positional words and develop spatial awareness with the help of a friendly bear. Place a cuddly little teddy bear (or other favorite stuffed animal) near a chair. In turn, help each child place the bear on, under, next to, behind, and in front of the chair. Then help him name the position of the bear. Teddy is under the chair!

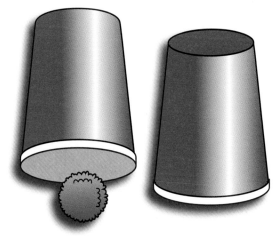

Watch That Cup!

Older toddlers practice tracking positions when they play this game. Gather two plastic cups and one pom-pom. Turn the two cups upside down on a tabletop. Encourage a youngster to watch closely as you place one of the cups over the pom-pom. Without lifting the cups, slide them on the table to change their positions. Then invite the child to tell you which cup she thinks the pom-pom is under. When she is ready for a further challenge, play the game using three cups.

Exploring the Senses

Little Ducks

Extend the fun of the favorite song "Five Little Ducks" at your water table. Obtain a set of rubber ducks, with one large duck to represent the mother. Give each child a duck. Move the mother duck around in the water; then encourage toddlers to make their ducks follow the mother duck as you sing the song together. Quack! Quack! Quack! All your little ducks will want to come back!

Let's Go Fishing!

Put in your water table a supply of plastic fish. Place near the table a plastic pail and several fishnets. Then invite a small group of youngsters to go fishing. Encourage each visiting child to scoop up a fish with a fishnet and put it in the pail. Once all the fish have been caught, invite one of your little fishermen to release them back into the water.

Ping-Pong Ball Scoop

Encourage your little ones to roll up their sleeves and have a ball at this "scooper-duper" water center. In advance, collect several plastic berry baskets and a supply of Ping-Pong balls. Float the balls in your water table. Then invite several children to each use a berry basket to scoop up the balls. Can she scoop just one ball? How many balls can she scoop at one time?

Simply Add Soap

It sounds simple—but it's so much fun! Plop a couple of bars of soap into your water table. For extra fun, add decorative soaps too! To provide a different type of sensory experience, include rubber kitchen gloves for little ones to wear while playing at this center.

Spoon, Shake, and Pour

Stimulate toddlers' senses of sight, hearing, and touch with this multisensory idea. Fill your sensory table with uncooked tinted rice. Add items such as spoons, detergent bottle caps, plastic jars with matching lids, and cardboard tubes to the table. Then invite youngsters to spoon, scoop, and pour the rice. For added fun, encourage a child to fill a jar about halfway; then help him screw the lid onto the jar. Now it's time to shake the jar and make some music!

Buried Treasures

Take your little explorers on a treasure hunt! Bury beneath the sand in your sensory table a variety of objects, such as large keys, plastic animals, and medium-size shells. Provide youngsters with plastic shovels for digging or encourage them to use both hands to search for buried treasures. For an added challenge, ask little ones to try to find matching treasures.

Sand Cakes

Little ones make size comparisons with this simple sensory idea. Dampen the sand in your sensory table. Add to the table a set of nesting cups, spoons, and birthday candles. Fill a cup with sand and then demonstrate how to make a cake from the mold. Then invite your little bakers to make cakes of their own and decorate them with birthday candles. Encourage youngsters to compare the sizes of the finished cakes, and then lead them in singing a chorus of "Happy Birthday to You."

Road Construction

Your sensory area will be humming with the sounds of bulldozers and backhoes when you add some road-construction props. Fill your sensory table with soil. Add some medium-size rocks and twigs, along with a supply of toy construction vehicles. Spray the soil with water to keep it moist and pliable; then watch your crew of workers dig in.

Find the Match

Use balls for this activity to develop the sense of touch and work on toddlers' perceptual skills. Gather a few pairs of small balls with different, interesting textures, such as two golf balls, two tennis balls, two Ping-Pong balls, and two foam balls. Put one ball from each pair in a "feely" box or a cloth bag, making sure they are covered so children can't see them. Then invite a child to choose one of the remaining balls. Have him reach into the box or bag to try to find the ball's match using only his sense of touch.

Mismatched Pairs

Try this matching game to stimulate toddlers' senses of touch and smell. Gather pairs of matching items, such as two rulers, two cube blocks, two bars of soap, and two cinnamon sticks. Place each item in a separate unmatched sock; then loosely knot the top of each sock. Place the socks containing matching items in each of two separate groups. Invite a child to examine a sock in one group. Then encourage her to examine each sock in the remaining group to find the one with the matching item. For younger toddlers, work with two pairs of socks at a time.

Mystery Sock

This idea that focuses on the sense of touch is just right for your older toddlers. Place a familiar object—such as a spoon, a rubber ball, or a small toothbrush—in a large plastic cup. Slide the cup into the bottom of an adult-size tube sock. Have a child slip her hand through the sock opening to feel the item in the cup. Then have her guess what the object is, providing clues as needed.

More Sticky Fun

Little hands won't have any trouble holding on to these shakers that stimulate the senses of hearing and touch. Partially fill oatmeal containers, cylindrical chip cans, or juice cans with rice or beans; then hot-glue on the lids. Tape a strip of Con-Tact covering around each container with the sticky side out. Give each child a sticky shaker to rattle as you play music. Not only will your little ones enjoy hearing the sounds of the shakers, they'll love the feel of the sticky paper as well!

Bubbles on Bubbles

For a sensory surprise, tape a large sheet of bubble wrap onto a tabletop. Squirt just enough dish detergent and water onto the wrap to create a slippery surface. Little hands will slip and slide for hours!

Freeze and Melt

Toddlers use their senses of touch and sight with this ice-cold experiment! In advance, fill an ice cube tray with water and tint each section with food coloring. Freeze the water; then place each ice cube in a separate resealable plastic bag, sealing the top of each bag with packing tape. Invite youngsters to manipulate the bags with their hands and then assist them in making observations as the ice cubes melt. If desired, place two different-colored ice cubes in each bag; then ask little ones what they see happening as the ice cubes melt.

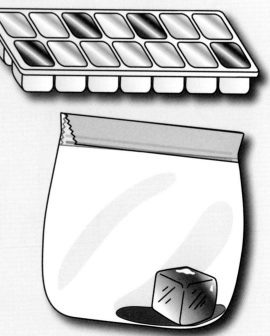

Appealing to the Senses

Children benefit from a variety of multisensory experiences, so try these multisensory exploration packs. Simply pour a desired amount of a substance suggested below into a resealable plastic bag. Squeeze as much air out of the bag as possible, seal it shut, and then reinforce the seal with packing tape. To use the pack, a child manipulates it with her hands or flattens it on a tabletop and draws on it with a finger.

Suggested substances for filling a pack: shampoo, hair gel, pudding, jelly, cooking oil with glitter, tinted glue, clear dish detergent with confetti

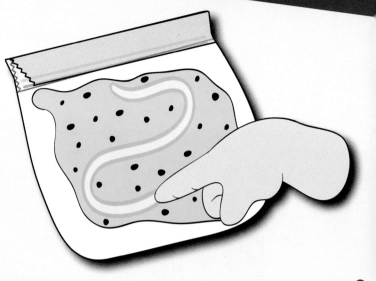

Blow, Blow, Blow!

With this idea, youngsters move an object without actually touching it! Invite a child to place a pom-pom at the edge of a small table. Encourage him to blow on the pom-pom, trying to make it fall off the opposite side of the table. Then invite him to try again, controlling his breath this time to blow softer or harder. Ask him to listen as he blows on the pom-pom. Does the air he breathes out sound different when he blows softer? Harder?

Singing the Senses

Here's a song that will leave you with an earful—of a sensory song, that is.

(sung to the tune of "Bingo")

We use five senses every day
To help us learn and play.
See, hear, smell, touch, taste.
See, hear, smell, touch, taste.
See, hear, smell, touch, taste.
We do these every day.

Songs, Rhymes, and Fingerplays

I Can See

This song will familiarize children with one another's names. Use a different child's name in each verse.

(sung to the tune of "Head and Shoulders")

I can see [Susie]'s here, [Susie]'s here.
I can see [Susie]'s here, [Susie]'s here.
Since she's here, I'll touch my ear.
I can see [Susie]'s here, [Susie]'s here.

I can see [Reina]'s there, [Reina]'s there.
I can see [Reina]'s there, [Reina]'s there.
Since she's there, I'll touch my hair.
I can see [Reina]'s there, [Reina]'s there.

I can see [Sam] is in, [Sam] is in.
I can see [Sam] is in, [Sam] is in.
Since he's in, I'll touch my chin.
I can see [Sam] is in, [Sam] is in.

Star Power

Welcome children to group time with this idea that is sure to make them feel like stars. Prepare by covering a class number of cardboard stars with foil. Give each child a star; then sing the following song until everyone has had a chance to shine.

(sung to the tune of "Twinkle, Twinkle, Little Star")

Twinkle, twinkle, little stars.
I'm so glad you're where you are!
When I say your name just right,
Hold your star up to the light.
[Courtney, Raymond,] little stars,
We're so glad you're where you are!

I Have Feelings

Help your youngsters learn to identify and express their feelings with this song. Invite students to use their voices, as well as body language, to dramatize the suggested feeling in the song. Then repeat the song, substituting a different feeling each time. In no time at all, your little ones will be singing about feelings.

(sung to the tune of "Frère Jacques")

I have feelings; I have feelings.
Look at me, and you'll see.
Sometimes I feel [mad],
Really, really [mad].
Look at me, and you'll see.

Feelings, Nothing More Than Feelings

What do you do when you feel the way you do? Discuss natural and appropriate behaviors associated with various feelings. Follow up your discussion with the following rhyme.

If I Were a Monster

If I were a happy monster, I'd go ha, ha, ha!
If I were a sad monster, I'd go boo, hoo, hoo.
If I were a mad monster, I'd go stomp, stomp, stomp!
If I were a scared monster, I'd go AAH! AAH! AAH!
But I'm just me, you see, so I'll go [sound or action of child's choice].

Thank you!

Good Manners Matter

It's never too early—or too late—to learn good manners! Teach your little ones this song to help promote and reinforce good manners.

(sung to the tune of "I'm a Little Teapot")

I have super manners. Yes, I do.
I can say please and thank you too.
When I play with friends, I like to share.
That's the way I show I care!

It's Snacktime!

This song's the signal. It must be snacktime!

(sung to the tune of "Frère Jacques")

Time for snack now.
Time for snack now.
Munch, munch, munch.
Crunch, crunch, crunch.
We will eat a little,
Just a little nibble.
Munch, munch, munch.
Crunch, crunch, crunch.

Keep 'em Clean

Keep this song handy throughout the year to remind students of a very healthful habit: washing hands!

(sung to the tune of "Row, Row, Row Your Boat")

Wash, wash, wash your hands
After work and play.
Scrub, rinse, shake, and dry.
Keep those germs away!

Brush Your Teeth

Sing the song below to inspire good brushing!

(sung to the tune of "Jingle Bells")

Brush your teeth.
Brush your teeth.
Give your teeth a treat.
Brush up and down and all around
To keep them clean and neat.

Ding, Ding, Ding!

Announce cleanup time to your little ones by ringing a bell. Then lead youngsters in singing this song. If desired, choose a different helper each day to ring the bell.

(sung to the tune of "Row, Row, Row Your Boat")

Ring, ring, ring the bell.
Ring it loud and clear.
Ring it out to let us know
Cleanup time is here!

Let's Get Together

Invite youngsters to join you for a special activity by singing the song shown. For added fun use a favorite classroom puppet.

(sung to the tune of "This Old Man")

Come join me, come join me
For a very special time!
Let's all gather round
And then we'll have some fun!
Please, come join me, everyone!

Hand Tricks

Use this nifty poem to get little ones ready before starting a group activity.

Clap your hands
Up high, down low.

Clap hands above head and then below waist.

Let them wobble
To and fro.

Wiggle hands.

Shake your hands;
Go left and right.

Shake hands to the left and the right.

Now tuck them in
Your lap so tight.

Fold hands in lap.

Wiggles

Use this fingerplay when you need a smooth transition from an active time to a quiet time.

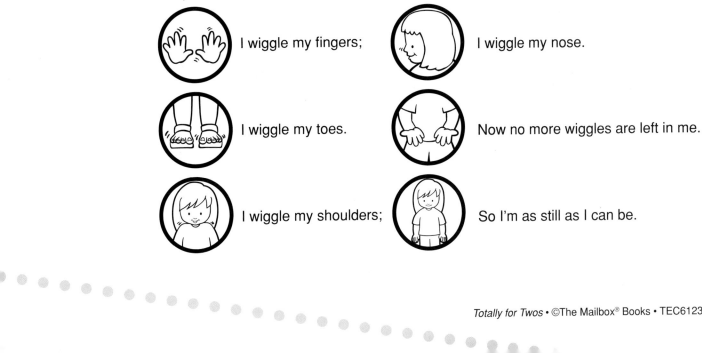

I wiggle my fingers;

I wiggle my nose.

I wiggle my toes.

Now no more wiggles are left in me.

I wiggle my shoulders;

So I'm as still as I can be.

What a Pair!

Hey! These hands really are handy. And these feet? Well, they just can't be beat! Sing this song and youngsters will soon recognize their terrific body-part twosomes. Encourage the group to name additional body-part pairs; then create new verses by adding a variety of movements.

(sung to the tune of "Bingo")

Oh, I have arms. I need my arms.
I use my arms all day, oh!
Arms, arms—swing those arms.
Arms, arms—swing those arms.
Arms, arms—swing those arms.
I use my arms all day, oh!

Continue with the following:
Hands, hands—clap those hands.
Legs, legs—wiggle those legs.
Feet, feet—stomp those feet.

This Is What I Can Do

Need to keep your little ones moving? Here's a catchy rhyme to pass on to your youngsters!

This is what I can do.   *Leader demonstrates a movement—stomping feet, etc.*
Everybody do it too!   *Group copies leader's movement.*
This is what I can do.
Now I'll pass it on to you!   *Point to new leader.*

Reach Up High, Reach Down Low

Youngsters understand high and low sounds best when moving! So get ready to move your body and the sound of your voice to match this action rhyme. For added fun, encourage little ones to stretch up as you play a xylophone so that the tones move up; then encourage youngsters to move their bodies downward as you play the instrument so that the tones move down.

Reach up high.
Reach down low.
Round and round and round we go.
Climb up high, up to the top.
Way back down we fall—kerplop!

Use a high voice.
Use a low voice.

Gradually use a higher voice.
Gradually use a lower voice.

Bubbles, Bubbles Everywhere

Following some outdoor bubble-blowing fun, encourage your little ones to "float" around like bubbles as you lead them in chanting the poem shown. At the end of the poem, have youngsters clap their hands to pretend they are popping bubbles and then sit quickly on the ground!

Bubbles, bubbles everywhere,
Floating gently through the air.
Let's all count: one, two, three.
Pop your bubbles now with me!

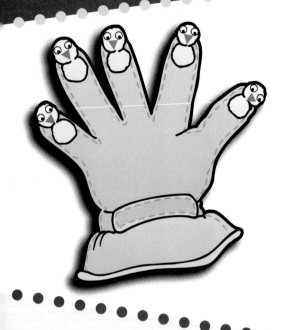

Give the Ducks a Hand

Captivate your toddlers' attention with this handy duck puppet. To make one, hot-glue two yellow pom-poms (duck head and body) to each fingertip on the palm side of a gardening glove. Glue two white mini pom-poms (eyes) to each duck head; then draw a black dot in the middle of each eye. To complete the puppet, glue an orange construction paper triangle beak to each head. Then don your puppet and sing "Five Little Ducks" with your children. Each time a duck is lost, fold a finger toward your palm. Then pop your fingers back up when the five little ducks return. Quack, quack, quack, quack, quack!

Did You Ever See a Fishy?

Did you ever see a fishy swim up and down? How about back and forth or around and around? Give each child a large fish cutout. Designate a pair of movements each time you sing the song shown. Then lead your little school of fish to swim this way and that.

(sung to the tune of "Did You Ever See a Lassie?")

Did you ever see a fishy, a fishy, a fishy?
Did you ever see a fishy swim this way and that?
Swim this way and that way and that way and this way,
Did you ever see a fishy swim this way and that?

A Shopping Song

Display several different plastic foods and then help little ones name each item. Next, lead youngsters in singing the first verse of the song shown. When the verse ends, invite a child to choose a food. Then lead children in singing the remaining verse, naming the chosen food.

(sung to the tune of "The Farmer in the Dell")

A-shopping we will go.
A-shopping we will go.
We need good food so we can grow.
A-shopping we will go.

Let's look for [bread] up high.
Let's look for [bread] down low.
We need good food so we can grow.
A-shopping we will go!

Lions and Tigers and Bears, Oh My!

Elephants, seals, and monkeys too! Show toddlers pictures of animals they might see at the circus. Help them name each animal. Then use this sing-along to find out which animal each of your little ones would be if she were in the circus. After each verse, invite toddlers to dramatize the choice.

(sung to the tune of "For He's a Jolly Good Fellow")

If [child's name] were in the circus,
If [child's name] were in the circus,
If [child's name] were in the circus,
[An animal] she would be.

Camping Trip

Have any of your little ones ever been camping? Have them tell about their adventures. Better yet, invite a parent to bring camping supplies—such as a sleeping bag, backpack, and flashlight—to your class. Include each item discussed below.

(sung to the tune of "Brush Your Teeth")

We're going on a camping trip, and what will we bring?
We're going on a camping trip, and what will we bring?
We'll bring a [tent]. *(clap, clap, clap, clap, clap, clap, clap, clap, clap)*
We'll bring a [tent]. *(clap, clap, clap, clap, clap, clap, clap, clap, clap)*

Weather Watcher

Just before your outdoor playtime, lead youngsters in singing this simple weather song. Then invite a child to look out the window and answer the question at the end of the song.

(sung to the tune of "Jingle Bells")

Sunny day,
Cloudy day,
Or rainy day so gray?
Look outside and tell us now:
Can we go out to play?

What's the Weather?

Lead your little weather watchers in reciting the poem below that is most appropriate for the weather.

Today we can go outside
And have a lot of fun,
Because today's weather
Calls for **sun.**

Arch arms overhead.

Today we'll put on hats and coats
To make sure we don't sneeze,
Because today's weather
Calls for a **breeze.**

Gently wave arms and blow.

Today we'll look up in the sky
To see white puffs in crowds,
Because today's weather
Calls for **clouds.**

Make a circle with hands over head.

Today we'll watch the water
Splash on the windowpane,
Because today's weather
Calls for **rain.**

Wiggle fingers downward.

Today we'll dress up warmly
To watch the white flakes blow,
Because today's weather
Calls for **snow.**

Slowly bring hands down.

Art Exploration

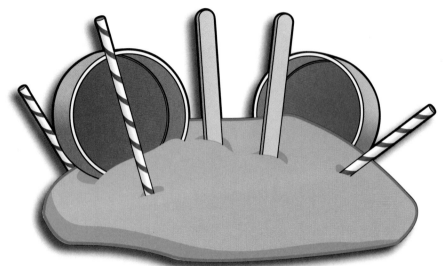

One-of-a-Kind Sculpture

Let the creativity begin! Place at a table a batch of play dough along with a variety of reusable items, such as large jug lids, metal lids from frozen juice concentrate, straws, and craft sticks. Encourage a child to press the materials of his choice into a lump of play dough to create an eye-catching masterpiece.

Drizzle Art

Toddlers explore the uniqueness of glue during this creative process. Tint several containers of white glue by mixing in tempera paint or food coloring. Place the glue at your art center along with a plastic spoon for each container and a supply of large tagboard shapes. Invite a child to use a spoon to drizzle glue onto a shape. Then encourage him to repeat the process with each remaining color.

The Yellow Pages

Need a unique art technique? Look in the yellow pages! Reuse old telephone books by removing the yellow pages. Encourage youngsters to tear the pages and then glue them to black construction paper. You'll be able to call these collages one-of-a-kind!

Ready to Make Purple?

Your little artists will love letting their creative juices flow with this fun idea. On a clean table in front of each child, place dabs of red and blue washable paint. Ask him what he thinks will happen when the two colors are mixed. Have each student use his hands to mix the two colors together. Encourage each child to use his fingers to make the design of his choice in the paint. When each child is satisfied with his creation, gently place a sheet of white construction paper atop his design. Rub your hand lightly over the entire paper. Lift the paper and let the paint dry.

Eraser Prints

Okay, your toddlers don't do paper-and-pencil work—but they can still use erasers! Purchase some of the fun theme-based erasers available at craft stores or teacher supply stores. Hot-glue each one to the end of an unsharpened pencil to make a stamp. Once the glue has cooled, add the stamps to your art area. Encourage each little one to press an eraser stamp into paint or onto an ink pad and then onto paper to make a design. This activity is sure to win your youngsters' stamp of approval!

Shoebox Shake

Here's a twist on that traditional favorite, golf ball painting. For each child, cut a sheet of white construction paper to fit inside a shoebox. Have a child dip a golf ball into paint and drop it into the box. Put the lid on the box; then wrap a large rubber band around the box to keep the lid securely in place. Instead of having the child tilt the box back and forth, have him shake it. Then open the box to observe the effect. Invite the child to add other paint colors. Then set the paper aside to dry. Display this artwork for everyone to admire!

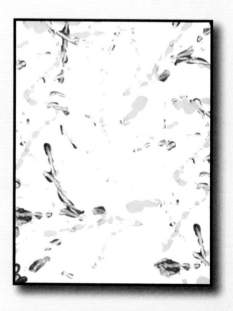

Tossed-Salad Art

In an art center, place cut vegetables and several containers of different-colored paint. Provide each child with a white paper plate. Help her dip one of the vegetables in the paint and press it onto the plate. Have her repeat this process using the various vegetables. To create a display, cover a table with a green paper tablecloth. Tape the dry vegetable prints to the tablecloth along with a sign titled "Tossed-Salad Art."

Dandy Prints

Use a bunch of blossoms to make dandelion prints. To prepare, pour yellow tempera paint in a tray. Clip several dandelion stems to about an inch below the flower. Then invite each child to dip a dandelion into the yellow paint and lightly press it onto a sheet of green paper. Encourage her to repeat the process several times so that the prints resemble dandelions growing in the grass.

Tubular Designs

Cut strips into one end of a cardboard tube; then bend the strips outward as shown. Instruct a child to dip the cut end into a shallow plate of paint and then press, tap, or twist the tube on a sheet of paper until he is satisfied with his work.

Chalk Art

Budding artists show off their creativity and develop prewriting skills with this idea. Provide sidewalk chalk and a small container of liquid, such as water, white tempera paint, liquid starch, or milk. Invite a child to dip a piece of chalk in the liquid. Then have him draw with the chalk on a sheet of construction paper, dipping the chalk in the liquid as needed. (As an alternative, help him spread the liquid onto the paper before or after he draws with the chalk.) This technique intensifies the colors of the chalk and seals the colors so they do not rub off the paper.

No-Mess Collage

Inspire toddlers' artistic creativity without the mess! Place at a table a container with a variety of collage materials, such as craft feathers, tissue paper scraps, construction paper scraps, and craft foam shapes. For each child, peel the backing from a sheet of clear Con-Tact covering; then place the covering sticky-side up on a table. Encourage each child to press a variety of collage materials onto the covering. If desired, attach the projects to a window for a colorful display.

Roll It! Paint It!

This technique is just right for little hands! Mount a large sheet of white bulletin board paper to a tabletop. Place dollops of red, yellow, and blue paint on the paper. Then encourage each visiting youngster to use a small paint roller to spread the paint across the paper. Little ones will be fascinated by the results of mixing paint colors!

Pull and Press

Toddlers get a fine-motor workout when they make these free-form designs. In advance, obtain several rolls of different-colored craft tape. Invite two or three toddlers to join you at a table. Then cut or tear pieces of craft tape from each roll and lightly attach one end of the tape to the edge of the table. Simply have each toddler pull pieces of tape from the table and press them onto a sheet of construction paper however she desires.

Fabulous Flower

Pot scrubbers aren't just for cleaning pots anymore! To prepare for this activity, cut out a supply of large construction paper flower shapes. Provide one or two shallow containers of different-colored paint and a nylon pot scrubber for each color. Help a child dip a pot scrubber in paint and then press it onto a flower shape. Encourage him to repeat the process until he is satisfied with his work.

Cool Spool Jewels

Toddlers just love to dress up in shiny jewelry! Send a note to parents asking them to help you by sending in the inner spools from rolls of wrapping paper and ribbon. Cut the cardboard spools into shorter lengths. Then help little ones cover the spools with shiny foil or metallic wrapping paper. Your toddlers will love showing off their shiny new bracelets. Cool!

Handmade Hats

What toddler wouldn't want to add one of these fancy hats to her wardrobe? For each child, roll up the edge of a paper lunch bag to create a brim. Provide materials such as crepe paper, tissue paper scraps, pom-poms, craft foam shapes, and tinted glue. Then help each child decorate a bag using the materials of her choice. Once the projects are dry, invite little ones to don their new hats and march in a hat parade!

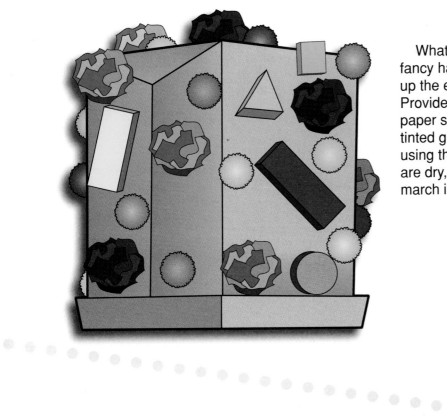

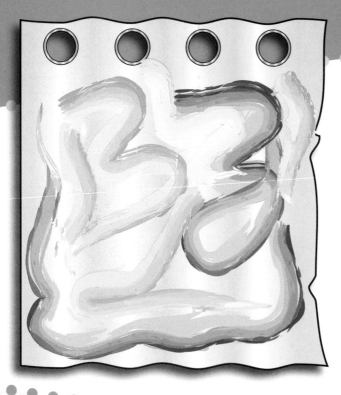

Shower Curtain Shimmy

Your toddlers will love this awesome combination of art and music! To prepare, cut a plastic shower curtain in half lengthwise; then attach one half to a tabletop. (Attach the remaining half to a second table or save it for another day.) Place several dollops of fingerpaint on the shower curtain. Then play a recording of lively music and have a small group of youngsters use their fingers to paint the shower curtain. Slide and swirl! Shimmy and shake!

Toe-Tapping Designs

Who says fingerpainting is just for fingers? In advance, obtain a supply of vinyl placemats. Place a protective covering on the floor where youngsters will be working; then put a placemat on top of the covering. Provide a chair, a tray with a shallow layer of paint, paper towels, and a plastic tub with soap and water for quick and easy cleanup. To prevent a child from slipping, have her sit on a chair and dip her bare feet in the paint. Then encourage her to paint a design on the mat by sliding her feet or tapping her toes!

Spool Tool

For this idea, you will need to collect several medium and large thread spools. (If none are available, use cardboard tubes instead.) Set out a desired number of paper plates, each with a shallow layer of paint. Help a child dip one end of a spool into paint and then press it onto a sheet of construction paper. Have him repeat the process, encouraging him to overlap the prints to create new colors and designs.

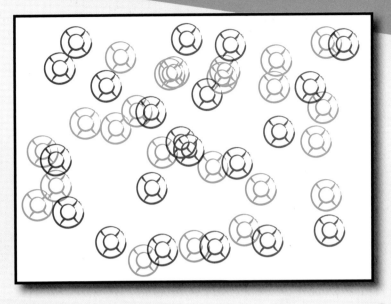

Shimmer and Shine

Use this simple mixture to create a dazzling effect! Tint separate containers of white corn syrup with different colors of neon food coloring. Place the containers at your easel with a paintbrush for each color. Then provide oversize shape cutouts for youngsters to paint with the shiny mixtures. Be sure to point out any changes that occur if the child mixes colors. Allow several days for the paintings to dry.

Squeeze and Dribble

This process art helps little ones build hand and finger muscles. In each of several separate bowls, mix equal parts of salt, water, and flour together until smooth and add several drops of food coloring. Then pour each mixture into a plastic squeeze bottle. Invite a child to squeeze the different mixtures onto a heavy paper plate. Then encourage her to fingerpaint with the gritty goop or provide a craft stick or spoon for manipulating the mixture. Allow several days for the projects to dry.

Lovely Lids

This creative craft inspires toddlers to experiment with movement and wind. Collect a supply of clean plastic lids from coffee cans or margarine tubs. Help each child glue crepe paper streamers to the edge of his lid. When the projects are dry, encourage each child to wave his project in the air to discover the movement of the streamers.

Cascade of Colors

To prepare, clip a cotton ball to each of several clothespins; then tape each clothespin above the cotton ball to keep the clothespin closed. Place the clothespins at a table along with several containers of tinted water and a supply of coffee filters. Demonstrate how to dip a cotton ball into a container of tinted water and then press it onto a coffee filter. Then help each toddler use the materials to create her very own cascade of colors. When the filters are dry, mount each one on a sheet of black construction paper for a brilliant effect!

3-D Appeal

A sculpted three-dimensional effect takes form with simple curling and gluing. To make a curly strip, tightly wrap a construction paper strip around a pencil; then remove the strip. Place a supply of curly strips at a table with a container of glue and glue brushes. Then help each child glue the curly strips to a sheet of construction paper. Now that's artwork that really stands out!

Gross-Motor Development

Toddler Parade

Learning to balance can be tricky! So give your little ones practice by having a parade. Prepare a masking tape trail on the floor in an open area. Have your toddlers follow you in parade fashion as you walk on the trail. Or travel to the beat of a lively selection of music. Ask an adult volunteer to stop the music to cue your group to freeze. Be sure to observe and take note of how well each of your toddlers balance on the line, both while walking and standing still.

Step-by-Step

Here's another quick way to have toddlers follow your lead to improve their walking skills. With a small number of youngsters behind you, take *giant steps, tiny steps, soft steps, stomping steps, skating steps,* and more. With every small step a toddler takes, there's a giant step toward gross-motor development!

Watch Out for Bigfoot!

If your toddlers like to try on adult-size shoes (and what toddler doesn't?), they'll love this activity that helps develop locomotor movements! To prepare, cover a piece of cardboard with colorful Con-Tact covering. Then trace adult-size footprints onto the paper and cut them out. Tape the cutouts to the bottom of a child's shoes and then invite him to walk, march, and stomp around the room with the big feet on. It's a clown...it's an elephant...no, it's toddler bigfoot!

Dot-to-Dot

Once your little ones get pretty good at moving around, prepare this game to help them learn to control their movements. For each child, secure a colorful, laminated construction paper circle to the floor in an open area. Direct each child in your group to stand on a circle. On your sound cue (such as a ringing bell or buzzer), challenge each child to move off his circle and onto a different circle by the time you give the cue a second time. Speed up the game or slow it down to match your children's abilities and interest levels.

Climbing the Wall

Work out little ones' shoulders and arms with this creative painting activity. Vertically attach a length of bulletin board paper to a wall so that the base of the paper is even with the base of the wall. Spread additional paper on the floor to protect it from paint. Have a child dip her hands into a shallow pan of washable paint. Direct the child to squat in front of the paper on the wall and to press her hands on the paper directly in front of her. Then challenge her to "walk" her hands up the paper as far as she can reach, leaving handprints that show her path.

Tiny Statues

This body-awareness activity helps little ones focus and develop muscle control as they copy specific body movements. Begin by having children sit on the floor with enough space between them to extend their arms to the sides without touching another child. Sitting on the floor and facing youngsters, extend your arms in a specific position. Encourage little ones to copy your pose. As children become familiar with the game, move from simple sitting poses to more complex standing poses.

Make Way!

Follow up a reading of Robert McCloskey's *Make Way for Ducklings* with this "quacked-up" version of Follow the Leader. Lead toddlers in practicing different ducky movements, such as waddling, wing-flapping, swimming, splashing, and bug-catching. Then, in turn, ask each of your darling ducklings to demonstrate a ducky movement of her choice while her classmates follow along.

Busy Bears

This action rhyme will exercise toddlers' listening skills as well as their ability to start and stop on cue. Using rhythm sticks, tap four steady beats after each line of the rhyme. Encourage little ones to add movements during your tapping and to stop the movements when you stop tapping. As youngsters become familiar with the rhyme, recite and tap a little faster. Start slowly—then look at those busy bears go!

Busy bears, busy bears, turn around.
Busy bears, busy bears, jump up and down.
Busy bears, busy bears, walk to me.
Busy bears, busy bears, bend your knees.
Busy bears, busy bears, touch your toes.
Busy bears, busy bears, tap your nose.
Busy bears, busy bears, hop around.
Busy bears, busy bears, sit on the ground.

Flashlight Dance

Heard of flashlight dancing? It's soon to be the craze on the toddler dance floor! Turn off several lights so the room is dim but not dark. Then turn on a flashlight and some lively music. Encourage youngsters to move in a manner similar to the movement of the flashlight. For example, if the light is moving rapidly up and down, encourage little ones to bounce. If the light is making a circular motion, encourage youngsters to move their arms, legs, or whole bodies in circles. Flashlight dancing…what a bright idea!

Wiggle Worms

Wiggle this movement idea right into your classroom! Have each child lie on his tummy with his arms at his sides. Then encourage him to crawl across the floor by wiggling his body like a worm. For added fun, invite each little worm to wiggle his way through an empty box, pretending he is crawling underground.

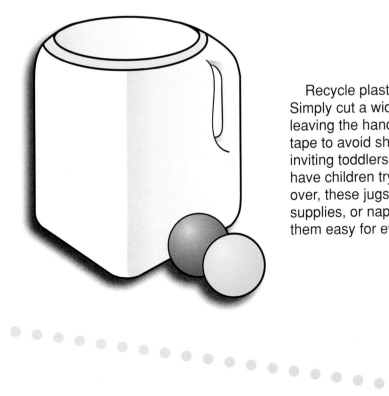

Got Milk Jugs?

Recycle plastic gallon milk jugs for a variety of classroom uses. Simply cut a wide circle around the spout of a clean milk jug, leaving the handle intact. Reinforce the cut edge with masking tape to avoid sharp edges. Use the jugs for tossing games, inviting toddlers to toss and catch beanbags or sponge balls. Or have children try to bounce balls into the jugs. When game time's over, these jugs are handy for carrying small manipulatives, craft supplies, or napkins and cups at snacktime. The handles make them easy for even the youngest toddlers to tote!

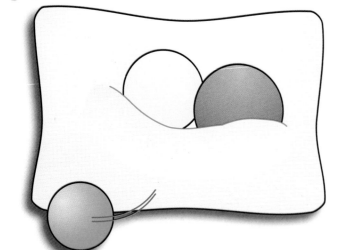

Runaway Balls

This silly activity will have your toddlers laughing, cooperating, *and* getting their exercise! Gather one or two fluffy bed pillows and some beach balls or large playground balls. Explain to a group of youngsters that the balls are tired and need to rest. Ask each child to put a ball on a pillow. (As one ball touches another on a pillow, one will roll off, making it difficult to put several balls on a pillow at one time.) Encourage youngsters to chase down the rolling balls and try again to "put them to bed." Good luck!

Strike!

This bowling game is inexpensive to prepare and is sure to have each of your toddlers on a roll toward improving large-motor movement and eye-hand coordination. Use markers to draw silly faces on six to eight empty, large, plastic soda bottles. Arrange these bottles in a close line or in a group. Challenge a child to roll a ball toward the bottles to see how many he can knock down. Take away one bottle at a time so that the child must roll more accurately in order to hit the remaining bottles.

Jumbo Ring Toss

Put some *big* rings into *little* hands for this active game that develops aim. Purchase a few 12-inch or 14-inch foam rings from your local craft store. If desired, decorate the rings with scarves or wide ribbon to make them more colorful. Provide a very large tub or box as a target. Ask children to toss the rings into the tub or box from increasingly greater distances. Ring a bell as each one lands in the target to signal success. Once little ones are proficient at tossing the rings into a tub or box, obtain a few small rubber traffic cones. Encourage toddlers to try to toss the rings on top of the cones. Ready…aim…toss!

Tunnel Ball

To make an outdoor obstacle course for toddlers to roll and kick balls through, collect a number of medium-size boxes without lids. Invert each box and cut tunnel-shaped holes through both ends. Arrange the boxes in a path in an open area. Then challenge youngsters to maneuver balls through each box.

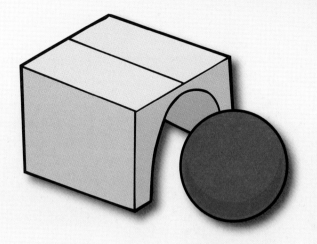

Geometric Bounce

Youngsters learn to bounce a ball inside a target and develop shape awareness with this simple idea. Use sidewalk chalk to draw large shape outlines—such as a circle, square, flower, and fish—on a concrete surface. Encourage each child to bounce a ball inside a shape.

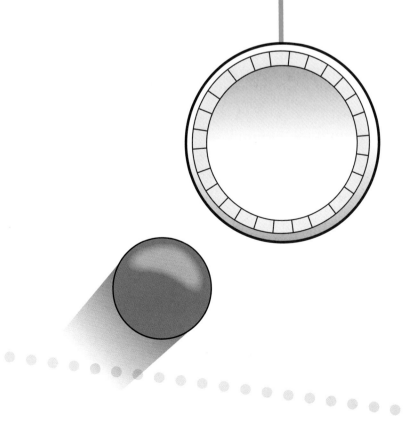

Dangling Targets

Little ones develop throwing skills with this fun activity. Punch holes in the rims of several pie tins. Use heavy string to dangle them from outdoor play equipment. Then provide balls for youngsters to throw at the tins. To help toddlers develop striking skills, provide them with cardboard tubes for hitting the pie tins. Ping!

Sock Toss

Toddlers take aim with this fun activity! To prepare, roll several socks into ball shapes. Place a laundry basket a few feet away from a marked start line. Invite a toddler to stand on the line and toss each sock into the laundry basket. As youngsters develop their tossing skills, move the basket farther away from the line.

Book Beams

Little ones practice walking and balancing with this homemade balance beam. Collect several same-size telephone books. Wrap each phone book with grocery bag paper and then secure the paper in place. Lay the phone books end to end on the floor. Then invite youngsters to walk across this makeshift balance beam that is just perfect for toddlers!

Nest, Sweet Nest

Watch motor skills take flight when using this idea. Give each child a toy hoop (nest) to place on the floor. Ask youngsters to imagine they are birds. Announce simple directions, such as "Walk around your nest" and "Hop inside your nest." At the conclusion of the activity, have your little birds settle down in their nests.

Animal Antics

There's plenty of room at the zoo for you and your youngsters when you participate in this fun action rhyme. Have little ones practice the way different zoo animals might move. Then recite the rhyme shown. At the end of the rhyme, encourage toddlers to move like the animal that was named. Repeat the rhyme several times, naming a different animal each time.

This is the way to the zoo.
This is the way to the zoo.
The [monkey] house is almost full,
But there's plenty of room for you.

Pass and Drop

Have little ones put on their listening ears to play a game that helps develop passing skills. Obtain a ball; then seat a small group of youngsters in a circle with their legs crossed. Encourage toddlers to pass the ball around the circle as you recite the rhyme shown. At the end of the rhyme, the child passing the ball drops it in the lap of the child sitting next to her. Continue until each child has had a turn to drop the ball in a classmate's lap.

Bip, bop, boop, bap!
Passing a ball is a snap.
Bip, bop, boop, bap!
Drop the ball right in a lap.

Beach Ball Bounce

With this fun idea, toddlers exercise their arm muscles and learn to work with a partner. Pair youngsters; then give each pair a beach towel. Have the children in each pair face each other and tightly hold the corners of their towel so it is extended. Then place a beach ball on the towel. Have little ones shake the towel up and down to bounce the ball in the air. Pick up and put back into play any balls that fall on the ground.

Tubular Obstacle Course

Tape a row of paper-towel tubes horizontally to the floor, leaving 12 inches of space between each tube. Have each child move from one end of the row to the other by performing a gross-motor skill—such as jumping, hopping, or walking—over the tubes.

Hopping Along!

Toddlers get plenty of practice hopping when they play this musical game. Scatter on the floor the same number of lily pad cutouts as there are children. Play a recording of lively music and encourage youngsters to pretend they are little frogs hopping around a pond. When you stop the music, encourage each of your little frogs to hop onto a lily pad. Happy hopping!

Jump the Brook

The fun of this large-muscle activity will make your little ones jump for joy, and the chance to review basic concepts, such as size and color, will make *you* jump for joy! Cut a supply of fish cutouts, reinforcing the concepts of your choice by varying the sizes or colors of the fish. Position two mats on the floor so that there is enough space between them for one fish. Describe the size or color of a fish as you place it between the mats; then invite each child, in turn, to jump the brook. Continue adding one fish at a time, moving the mats farther apart until the children can no longer jump the brook without the fish "nibbling" the jumpers' feet. Splash!

Scratch a Beat

With this idea, little ones strengthen their arm muscles as they make music. To begin, make rhythm blocks by stuffing miniature cereal boxes with newspaper. Then tape or glue sandpaper around each box. Give each child a pair of rhythm blocks and encourage him to rub the blocks together as he listens to favorite classroom tunes.

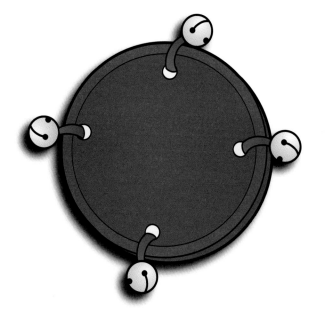

Tambourines for Tots

Save those lids! Small margarine tub lids can be used to make miniature tambourines. Punch three or four holes around the edge of the lid; then use short lengths of ribbon to tie a giant bell to each hole. Provide each child with a tambourine and play a lively musical selection. Invite your youngsters to shake their tambourines and dance to the beat of the music.

Fine-Motor Development

Lace Impressions

This dough activity will leave quite an impression on little ones! In advance, purchase a variety of inexpensive lace with large, distinct patterns. Place the lace at your play dough area. To use the center, a child rolls out the play dough, presses the lace in the dough, and then removes the lace. Look at that—a lace design in the dough!

Sudsy Sponges

The more hands the merrier when it comes to this sudsy activity! Fill an assortment of easy-to-squeeze sponges with tearless baby shampoo. Add just enough water to moisten the sponges and to get the bubbles started. Place the sponges in your water table or a large plastic tub. (Keep hand towels and a bucket of water nearby for easy cleanup.) When visiting the center, your little ones will know just what to do—squeeze!

Magnet Mania

Bring out your scissors to prepare this magnet activity that will build your tiny tots' dexterity. Cut flexible magnetic sheets into short and long pieces, as well as simple shapes and curvy lines. Stick the pieces onto cookie sheets and invite your youngsters to experiment!

Play Dough Party Place

Join the fun at the play dough party place where birthday cakes are the focus of fine-motor fun. Collect disposable tart pans, potpie tins, and muffin pans. Place the pans in a center along with play dough, birthday candles or cut straws, craft sticks or plastic knives, and festive paper plates. Let's make a cake!

Terrific Teeth

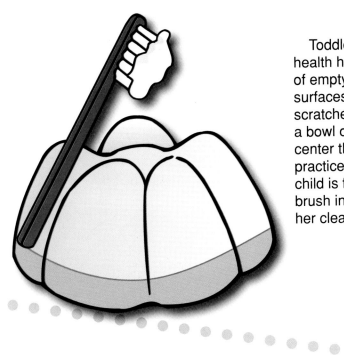

Toddlers develop fine-motor skills and important dental health habits with this "scrub-ulous" idea. Cut off the bottoms of empty one- or two-liter plastic bottles that resemble tooth surfaces. Tape the cut edges to protect your little ones from scratches. Place the plastic teeth, several toothbrushes, and a bowl of nonmentholated shaving cream (toothpaste) in a center that is located near a sink. Then invite little ones to practice their brushing skills on the plastic teeth. When each child is finished, have her rinse her plastic tooth and toothbrush in the sink so that another budding brusher can polish her cleaning skills.

Tube Tapping

Give this idea a whirl to help little ones strengthen their hand and finger grasp. Provide each child with a pair of cardboard tubes to use as rhythm sticks. Then invite little ones to tap their tubes together, on a table, or on the floor as you play a recording of music. To add to the fun, play a selection of music with a speedy beat and encourage your musical maestros to tap their tubes to the fast-paced tempo!

Stamp of Approval

Inspire toddlers' creativity with this simple fine-motor workout. Provide a variety of rubber stamps, colorful stamp pads, and paper. Demonstrate how to make a stamp print. Then invite youngsters to use the materials to create stamp prints of their own. For an added challenge, provide paper with a large shape outline—such as a circle, square, or heart—and invite more advanced toddlers to stamp pictures along the outline.

Stick 'em Up

Create a fine-motor center in your classroom by using your metal filing cabinets as magnet boards. Attach self-adhesive magnetic tape to items such as pattern blocks, puzzle pieces, felt shapes, photographs, empty product boxes, and more. The possibilities are unlimited!

Toddler Magic

"You can do it!" are the only magic words you'll need to encourage a child to give this scarf trick a try. To prepare, cover a large can that has a tight-fitting lid (such as a coffee can) with colorful Con-Tact covering. Cut an X in the lid to create an opening that is large enough for a toddler to put her hand through. Trim the sharp points of the lid. Have a child observe as you put a number of colorful scarves into the can through the lid. Then pull out one of the scarves and wave it in the air with great excitement. Pull out the tip of another scarf before offering the can to the child. For younger toddlers, tie the scarves together to make them easier to pull out. Forget Houdini! You're looking at the great "Two-dini"!

Hide-and-Seek

This idea uses a toddler's natural curiosity as a motivational tool for fine-motor fun. Fill a small tub with paper shreds. Put the tub and several objects—such as large beads, cubes, or toy cars—on the floor in front of a child. Begin by choosing one item and pushing it down into the paper shreds so that it is hidden from view. Invite the child to put his hand in the tub to find the object. Ask him to grasp the item and tell you what he feels, supplying words such as *soft, bumpy,* and *hard* as necessary. Gradually increase the number of items you put into the tub at one time. The look of delight on the child's face when his hand disappears into the shreds will let you know he's having fun and learning too!

Tunnel Tubes

Keep youngsters' hands busy with this tunnel-tube challenge. Invite each child to use markers and seasonal stickers to personalize a cardboard tube. Have the child use one hand to hold the tube horizontally at one end. Put a Ping-Pong ball in the tube; then challenge the child to balance her tube so that the ball does not roll out. As the child becomes better at managing this trick, have her gradually move her hand toward the center of the tube.

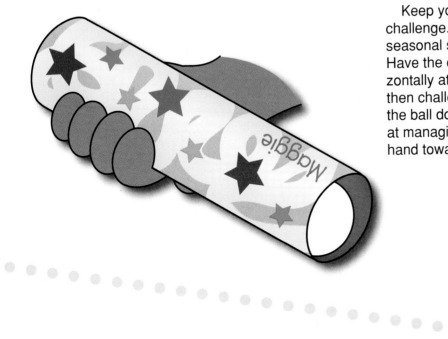

Hamburger Helpers

Toddlers mold play dough patties to cook on this makeshift grill! Provide a wire baking rack to represent a grill, along with other props such as an apron, a checkered tablecloth, paper plates, a spatula, and condiment squeeze bottles. Invite your little backyard chefs to press portions of play dough into hamburger-like patties and then "cook" them on the grill. Encourage youngsters to flip the burgers using the spatula to be sure they cook on both sides. Finally, invite tots to squeeze their favorite condiment onto their tasty burger!

Fill It Up!

Stand various-size cardboard tubes in the sand at your sand table. Put in the table several tools such as plastic spoons, powdered drink mix scoops, and measuring cups. Invite a visiting youngster to use the tools to pour sand in a tube until it is filled to the top. Once the tube is full, have her pull it out of the sand to empty it. Then encourage her to gently push one end of the tube back into the sand to make it stand. Fill it up!

Don't Trash Those Tops!

Get some punch out of those old plastic lids when you use them for lacing activities. Collect plastic lids from small microwave meals, margarine tubs, or coffee cans. Using a hole punch or a hammer and nail, make several large holes in each lid. For each lid, thread a shoelace through one of the holes; then secure one end of the lace to the lid with a knot. Help a child weave the shoelace through each hole. When the weaving is complete, help him remove the lace to ready it for the next child.

Picture-Book Puzzles

Don't toss out those books with missing or torn pages! Use the remaining pages to make puzzles. To make one puzzle, choose a page from the book that has a bright, interesting picture. Remove the page from the book and then glue it onto a piece of tagboard or poster board. Laminate the page and then cut it into large jigsaw puzzle pieces. Place the puzzle in a resealable plastic bag and set it near a replacement copy of the book. As little ones piece together the puzzle, they will be reminded of a familiar and favorite story.

Apple Picking

Youngsters develop their pincer grasps with this sweet idea! Attach the loop side of a supply of Velcro fasteners to a large poster board tree; then mount the tree on a wall. Attach the hook side of Velcro fasteners to a supply of tagboard apples; then fasten the apples to the tree. Give a child a basket and invite her to go apple picking. Encourage her to pull each apple from the tree and put it in the basket. When she is finished apple picking, have her put the apples back on the tree to ready it for the next apple picker.

Polka Dots Galore

Your little ones will become familiar with colors, as well as exercise their fine-motor muscles, when they make these colorful circles. Supply each child with a sheet of colorful circle stickers and a tagboard circle. Encourage her to peel the stickers from the sheet and then press them onto the circle. When she has peeled and pressed all her stickers, ask her to point to each dot and help her name its color.

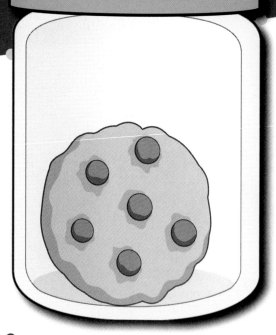

Who Took the Cookie From the Cookie Jar?

Toddlers can take the cookies from the cookie jar. Who, twos? Yes, twos! Remove the labels from a number of clean, large, clear plastic jars. Put an edible treat—such as a cookie or cracker—inside each jar; then loosely screw on the lid. Demonstrate how to unscrew the lid from a jar, take out the cookie inside, and screw the lid back on. (As children gain proficiency at this task, screw the lids on tighter.) Give each child a jar and encourage him to give the jar a twist to get his treat.

Shake Things Up

Learning to pick up and hold objects is an exciting accomplishment. To help your younger toddlers develop this skill, fill containers—such as potato chip cans and spice bottles—with dried beans, beads, or bells to make shakers. Tightly screw on the lids and secure them with tape. First, provide large shakers that need to be held with two hands; then gradually decrease the size of the containers to those that can be easily held by one hand. If room, give each child a shaker and play some lively music. Who would have thought that working on fine-motor skills would be so noisy and fun?

Drop Everything!

This activity develops imaginations and language skills, provides grasping and releasing practice, and builds self-esteem. Make a game out of picking up a group of like toys and dropping them into a tub by pretending that the tub is something different that relates to the items. For example, with a collection of plastic food, pretend the tub is a soup pot. Repeatedly encourage a child to pick up a toy food and drop it in the soup pot (tub). During the fun, describe the items and emphasize how they relate. Clap and praise the child each time she drops an object in the tub. Let's go now...grab and release, grab and release...

Are You Pulling My Bead?

No kidding! Children are sure to enjoy this game so much you'll almost be able to watch their minds figuring out how it works! To make one, punch four holes in a sturdy paper plate as shown. Thread an 18-inch length of yarn through each pair of holes; then tie a large wooden bead to each end of each length. To use the toy, a child pulls on one bead to make the bead at the opposite end of the yarn move. *How* does that work?

This Game's a Ringer

When it comes to developing hand-eye coordination, this activity is a ringer! Borrow a clean baby-bottle drainer. Then collect a number of plastic bracelets and have children put the bracelets on the drainer's posts. Encouraging children to put the bracelets on their wrists is yet another quick way to develop small-muscle coordination.

Spreading Some Skills

Toddlers can practice their coordination skills as they prepare their own simple snacks. Give each child a rice cake, a cracker, or a slice of toast on a napkin. Then provide him with a plastic knife and invite him to choose from a variety of spreads, such as softened butter, cream cheese, or jelly. What a delicious way to learn!

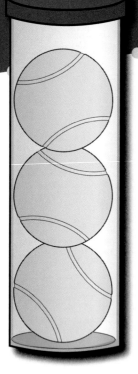

Tennis, Anyone?

Obtain a container of tennis balls. Invite a small group of youngsters to sit in a circle. Remove the tennis balls from the container; then place the empty container in the center of the circle. Play a recording of music and have youngsters pass one of the balls around the circle. When you stop the music, have the child holding the ball put it in the container. Repeat the process until each tennis ball is in the container and then invite a child to replace the lid.

Is It the Same Size?

Toddlers develop visual discrimination skills, eye-hand coordination, and fine-motor skills with this simple idea. Collect balls of various sizes and a lidded box that is large enough to hold all the balls at once. Cut holes in the sides of the box that correspond to the sizes of the balls. To use the activity, have a child match each ball to a hole and insert it into the box.

Tee Time!

To prepare for this activity, press a desired number of golf tees into a large piece of polystyrene foam. Provide little ones with a matching number of golf balls. To use, encourage a youngster to place a golf ball on top of each tee. To add matching skills to this fine-motor challenge, use colored tees and matching-colored golf balls.

Squirting With a Twist

Toddlers give their finger muscles a real workout when they participate in this outdoor activity! Place a few buckets, each filled with a different color of water, in a plastic pool or tub along with several turkey basters. Demonstrate for youngsters how to use a turkey baster; then invite them to give it a try. Little ones will be amazed to see that as they squirt the water, new colors are created.

Ping-Pong Ball Transfer

Little ones get plenty of hand and finger strengthening exercise with this idea. Place a container of Ping-Pong balls at a center along with an empty basket and a pair of salad tongs. Model how to use the tongs to pick up a Ping-Pong ball and transfer it to the basket. Then encourage a child to use the tongs to transfer the remaining balls to the basket.

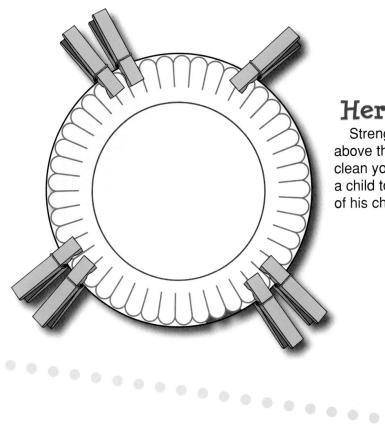

Here a Clip, There a Clip

Strengthen little fingers at this center that is a pinch above the rest. Stock a center with plastic clothespins, clean yogurt containers, and plastic plates. Encourage a child to fasten the clothespins to the rim of the item of his choice.

Fabulous Fall

Muddy Prints

This exploration activity is sure to interest your toddler scientists! On an autumn day, take little ones outdoors to collect twigs and leaves. Next, work with a small group of children to mix soil and water together in a shallow pan to make thick mud. Invite each child to press one of the natural objects on the mud to make an impression. Set the pan of mud and objects aside to harden for several days; then invite the group to pull off the objects to see the impressions left behind. What's next? Add water and make more mud!

Way Cool Watercolors!

Spread some autumn color with this no-mess paint palette! To prepare one, simply squirt small amounts of red, brown, orange, and yellow washable tempera paints onto a paper plate. Let the paint dry overnight. To paint, a child repeatedly wets his paintbrush in a cup of water, then brushes it across the dried paint to form a design on the plate. Younger tots may want to try fingerpainting wet fingers across the dried paints. Before you know it, your little ones will have created way cool shades of autumn color!

Take a Closer Look at Leaves

Ask your little ones to help you collect fallen leaves. Then, in turn, have each child help you press a number of the leaves onto the sticky side of a precut Con-Tact paper square to create a collage. (If you'd like to send the collages home later, save the paper backing from each square.) Help the child press the square to a low window, on a wall near a quiet area, on a mirror, or even on the floor. If desired, engage children in conversation as you notice them stopping to take a closer look at the leaves throughout your room all day long.

Catch a Falling Feather

Since older toddlers enjoy the challenge of catching things, give them practice with this colorful activity. Drop a handful of red, yellow, brown, and orange nonshedding feathers from above the heads of several children and encourage the children to pretend the feathers are leaves. Instruct children to bring their hands together to catch the slow-moving feathers. The colors are sure to excite them, and the whimsical movement of the falling feathers will entice them!

Leaf Catch

Your tiny tots are sure to catch on quickly to this leaf-dropping activity that develops gross-motor skills. To prepare, cut out several large hand shapes from laminated paper; then secure them to the floor. Provide a child with red, yellow, or orange beanbags. (Or tape paper leaf cutouts onto beanbags.) Ask the child to pretend that the beanbags are leaves and to drop them onto the hand cutouts so that they can be caught. As the child becomes more proficient with dropping the leaves, encourage him to stand a short distance from the cutouts and then toss the beanbags onto the hands.

Leaves Are Falling All Around!

Take youngsters on an outdoor leaf hunt. Or have them hunt for construction paper leaves hidden around your classroom. Follow up your leaf hunt with this action song that reinforces the signs of the fall season.

(sung to the tune of "London Bridge")

Leaves are falling all around—
Red,
Yellow,
Orange,
And brown.
Twirling, swirling to the ground—
It is autumn!

Wiggle fingers while moving arms up and down.

Twirl around like a falling leaf.
Gently fall to the ground.

Mr. Squirrel

Who's that scampering up the tree

Carrying acorns…1, 2, 3?

It's Mr. Squirrel with a tail so furry.

He's ready for winter, so don't you worry!

Bobbing Jack-o'-Lanterns

Your youngsters will have a ball when strengthening fine-motor skills at this seasonal center. Use a black permanent marker to draw jack-o'-lantern faces on a quantity of orange Ping-Pong balls; then float the balls in your water table. Place a fishnet (or large spoon) and a jack-o'-lantern bucket nearby. A child manipulates the net to scoop the jack-o'-lanterns and then drops them into the bucket.

Pumpkin Surprises

If your children enjoy "feely box" activities, try this seasonal twist. Put several objects in a plastic pumpkin. Show a child a treat such as a juice box; then put it in the pumpkin too. Have the child close his eyes and then reach into the pumpkin to find the treat by feeling instead of looking. There's no trick. This game's a treat!

Grinnin' Pumpkin Faces!

Keep toddlers grinning with this quick and simple art center idea. To make each pumpkin, cut a piece of orange tagboard to the dimensions of a resealable plastic bag. Use a black marker to draw a simple pumpkin outline on the tagboard; then seal the tagboard in the bag. Invite a child to use a dry-erase marker to draw lines and squiggles on the bag to give the pumpkin a silly face or a jack-o'-lantern grin. When she is finished, have her simply use a tissue to wipe off the bag.

Pack of Pumpkin "Stuff"

Tell your little ones that these bags are full of squishy pumpkin "stuff," and they'll be eager to give their fingers a no-mess, fine-motor workout! To prepare each pumpkin pack, put a spoonful each of yellow and red paint into a resealable plastic bag. Place packing tape along the top of the bag to ensure it stays closed. Give a child a bag to squish until it is filled with orange paint instead of red and yellow. Next, give him a black construction paper workmat. Encourage him to put his bag on the mat and then use his fingers to draw designs in the paint.

Jack-o'-Lantern Mystery

This quick and simple jack-o'-lantern game will keep 'em thinking and grinning! From orange and black felt, cut out a pumpkin shape and jack-o'-lantern facial features. Put all the pieces on a flannelboard; then use them to play a What's Missing? game. Once the children are familiar with the game, vary it by asking a different child each time to take away a piece. Or make it more challenging by adding more felt pieces such as a stem, a leaf, or teeth for the grin.

Meow!

Halloween Pretending

Each time you sing this song, invite a student to pretend to be the character of her choice. Pretending is fun!

(sung to the tune of "Clementine")

Halloween is such a fun time.
It's not scary, not for me.
I pretend I'm someone different.
It's as fun as fun can be.

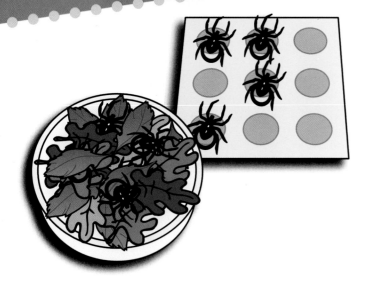

Sorting and Counting Seasonal Stuff

Here's a use for inexpensive fall decorations, such as silk leaves, spider rings, and turkey feathers. Prepare a sorting mat by drawing nine large dots on a piece of poster board as shown. Place the assortment of objects in a container. Working with one or two children at a time, ask a child to put one spider on each dot, for example. The child then sorts through the items, putting one spider on each dot each time he finds one. For toddler math practice, this seasonal activity hits the spot!

Seasonal Sensation

What's orange and black and creeping with spiders? The contents of your sensory table are when you fill it with orange and black shredded paper and a quantity of plastic spiders. Encourage a child to find the spiders and then return them to the table.

Profile Puzzles

Shape up visual-discrimination skills with these fun puzzles. Gather collections of items. Arrange each collection on a piece of poster board; then use a black marker to trace around each item's shape. Laminate if desired. A child places each object from a collection on its corresponding outline.

Vine Times

Toddlers develop balance and coordination when they walk along this faux pumpkin vine! Use wide masking tape to mark a meandering vine on the floor in an open area of your room. Embellish the vine with a few construction paper leaves; then place a supply of pumpkin cutouts near one end of the vine so it resembles a pumpkin patch. Encourage each child to walk along the vine without stepping off, and provide help as needed. When the child reaches the pumpkin patch, invite her to pick a pumpkin to decorate in your art area.

Funny Scarecrows

Got a field that needs guarding? Enlist the help of your little ones as they participate in this fun fall poem. Ask your floppy friends to name a different body part to wiggle each time you recite the rhyme.

The funny, funny scarecrow
Guards the field all day.
It waves its floppy, floppy [arms]
To scare the crows away!

Getting a Feel for Vegetables

Challenge a small group of youngsters with this fun guessing game. Pass around a few vegetables for little ones to look at and feel, such as a potato, a carrot, and a small pumpkin. Help toddlers name each item as they examine it; then place the foods in a shopping bag. In turn, invite each child to reach into the bag and feel an item. Encourage him to guess which item it is, reminding him of the food names if needed. Then have him remove the item from the bag to reveal its identity.

Twinkle Toes the Turkey

Twinkle Toes the turkey will keep little ones moving while helping them learn to follow directions. To prepare, cut out a large tagboard turkey and several tagboard feathers. Write simple directions on each feather, such as "Stamp your feet" or "Touch your nose." Attach the hook side of a Velcro fastener to each feather and the loop side of a Velcro fastener to the turkey's tail. Mount the turkey to the lower portion of a wall; then attach the feathers to the turkey. To play, invite a volunteer to remove a feather from the turkey's tail. Read aloud the directions and encourage the group to perform the action.

Mr. Pumpkin and Mr. Turkey

Lead your little ones in singing these fun verses in honor of Mr. Pumpkin and Mr. Turkey. Harvesttime is coming! Yum, yum, yum!

(sung to the tune of "Frère Jacques")

Mr. Pumpkin,	Mr. Turkey,
Mr. Pumpkin,	Mr. Turkey,
Round and fat,	Round and fat,
Round and fat.	Round and fat.
Harvesttime is coming.	Dinnertime is coming.
Harvesttime is coming.	Dinnertime is coming.
Yum, yum, yum.	Yum, yum, yum.
Yum, yum, yum.	Yum, yum, yum.

Turkeys in the Nest

To play this game, place several large plastic hoops (nests) on the floor in an open space. Have youngsters pretend to be turkeys by moving around the nests flapping their arms, scratching the floor with their feet, and saying, "Gobble, gobble, gobble." After a few moments announce, "Turkeys in the nest!" to signal your little turkeys to each sit in a nest. Encourage toddlers to cooperate and share their nests with their fellow turkeys.

Read All About It!
Our Class News

Read All About It!
Our Class News

Note to the teacher: Program a newsletter as desired; then send a copy home with each youngster.

Wonderful Winter

How Do You Celebrate?

Different families have different holiday traditions. Use this simple home-to-school connection and invite parents to share their special traditions with your class. To begin, use a cassette player to record yourself describing some ways you and your family celebrate the holidays. Next, write a note to parents explaining the project and inviting them to briefly describe some of their family's holiday traditions. Send home the note, tape, and tape player with each child in turn. After each child returns the tape, play her family's holiday account for the class. When the tape is complete, play it during naptime or other quiet times to soothe your tots with familiar voices and holiday recollections.

Sweet Holiday Scents

Invite your tots to follow their noses with this idea. In advance, gather a variety of holiday treats with distinctive scents, such as a gingerbread cookie, hot chocolate mix, and a peppermint stick. Invite each child to smell the items and become familiar with the different scents. Then place each item in a separate paper bag. Hold the bag so the opening is closed almost all the way. Have a child sniff the contents of the bag without looking inside it; then ask him to identify the smell. Afterward, reward each child by allowing him to choose one of the tasty treats to sample. Hot chocolate, please!

Busy With Bows

Toddlers get a gross-motor workout and develop listening skills with this fun idea! Scatter a supply of gift bows in an open area of the classroom floor. Then encourage little ones to walk around the bows, trying not to step on them. After a few moments, ring a pair of bells to signal youngsters to stop. Continue the activity in the same way, substituting a different gross-motor movement each time. When it's time to clean up, place a gift-wrapped box on the floor; then encourage each child to pick up a bow and toss it into the box.

Gorgeous Gift Wrap

Stock your art center with holiday cookie cutters, colorful stamp pads, and a supply of newsprint. Then help each child create decorative paper that can be used as personalized gift wrap.

Reindeer Romp

Display a picture of Santa and his reindeer. Ask youngsters how they think the reindeer move. Help them name movements such as walking, running, jumping, leaping, galloping, prancing, and flying. Next, provide each child with an antler headband. Then invite little ones to pretend they are Santa's reindeer, and lead them around the room trying all these gross-motor movements—except flying, that is!

Santa's Beard Is Soft and White

Your little merrymakers will get a real feel for Santa's beard when visiting this tactile center. Enlarge the Santa pattern from page 108 onto a large sheet of white paper. Color the pattern. Tape it on a tabletop; then cover it with clear Con-Tact covering. Squirt a dollop of nonmenthol-scented shaving cream onto Santa's beard. Invite a child to use her fingers to give Santa a beard that is fluffy and white.

Holiday Highlights

Parents will appreciate this keepsake, and it also makes a nice conversation piece for holiday visitors. Several days before your winter break, trace around each child's body on a length of bulletin board paper. Each day, have the child color in a little bit of his body outline as you talk with him about various body parts, his hair color, his eye color, and so on. Next to each outline, write in some vital statistics, such as the child's height, weight, current interests, favorite stories, or favorite activities. Send the finished projects home before the holidays. What a wonderful memory of the year!

Elfin Excursion

Your youngsters are sure to be thrilled when you ask them to be Santa's helpers for this hide-and-seek game! To prepare, wrap several empty boxes in holiday paper and ribbon. Hide the boxes in easy-to-spot places in your play yard or play area. Then explain to your little ones that Santa has lost some gifts and needs their help to find them. Give clues as needed until all the gifts are rounded up. Play the game again on subsequent days, increasing the difficulty of the hiding places as youngsters get better at finding the gifts.

Handsome Holiday Decorations

Dress up any holiday table with this handmade craft! To make one, invite a child to choose a sheet of colored construction paper; then label the paper with his name. Next, cover the palm of his hand with white paint and have him make a handprint on the center of the paper. Turn the paper in a clockwise direction; then have the child make another handprint that slightly overlaps the first one. Continue in this manner until the child's handprints resemble a snowflake in the center of the paper. If desired, have the child sprinkle Epsom salts onto the wet paint to add a little sparkle to the snowflake. When the paint is dry, laminate the paper to create a perfect holiday placemat or centerpiece.

Cory

Wish Upon a Star

While young children are often eager to recite their own Christmas wish lists, they may need a little coaxing to consider the wishes of family and friends. Share the poem below; then ask your youngsters what they would wish for family members or friends.

I wish upon a star,   *Clasp hands and look up.*
The first star that I see.   *Point up to the sky.*
One wish is for you,   *Point out.*
And the other is for me!   *Point thumb toward self.*

I Am a Little Dreidel

Why not give this holiday poem a spin?

I am a little dreidel.	*Point to yourself.*
I am a little top.	*Pat your head.*
When you twist my handle,	*Spin around.*
I spin until I drop!	*Fall to the floor.*

Kwanzaa Candles

Use this poem as a fingerplay or to introduce a real *kinara* (candleholder) and the *mishumaa saba* (seven candles) used during Kwanzaa.

Seven little candles all in a line,
Waiting to be lit at Kwanzaa time.
Come, let's count them—one, two, three,
Four, five, six, seven candles I see!

Give a Cheer for the New Year!

Provide your little ones with some bells and drums so they can ring and tap along as you sing this New Year's song!

(sung to the tune of "Row, Row, Row Your Boat")

Ring, ring, ring the bells.
Tap, tap, tap the drums.
The new year's here.
Let's give a cheer.
We'll have a year of fun!

Freeze! Melt!

Increase your toddlers' muscle control with this wintry stop-and-go game. Prepare a large sun cutout and a large snowflake cutout. Hold the snowflake in the air and have each child pretend to be a snowman frozen in the cold winter snow. Next, hold the sun in the air and encourage each child to slowly move like she is melting in the warm sun. Then hold the snowflake in the air to signal youngsters to freeze in place again. Continue in the same way until all your little snowmen have melted to the ground. Little ones are sure to enjoy this game all winter long!

Make a Snowstorm

Don't toss out that crumpled tissue paper that's left over in gift boxes after the holiday unwrapping! Put it to good use to make some faux snow that's soft and safe. Invite your little ones to scrunch the tissue up into small balls. When you have a tub full, let the snowballs shower down on some delighted toddlers! Encourage youngsters to toss these fake snowballs, pour them onto the floor and take a walk through the snowdrift, or try to make snow angels in them! When they're done with the snowy fun, just sweep it up!

Mmmm! Warm!

After an outdoor play period, warm up little hands and tummies with this tasty treat. While your youngsters are outside, have an adult volunteer make a batch of cooked pudding that will be ready to eat when students return to the room. Provide each child with an ice cream cone; then spoon some of the warm pudding into the cone. As your little ones hold their cones, lead them to notice that the warm pudding warms the cone, which warms their hands! Invite your youngsters to eat their pudding cones and let the pudding warm them from their taste buds to their tummies!

Everything Snowballed!

Has the dreary winter weather trapped your little ones inside? If so, use this indoor snowball activity to chase away those winter blues and exercise gross-motor skills! To prepare, blow up a class supply of small white balloons; then place each one inside a white knee-high stocking. Tie a secure knot in the end of each stocking. (If a balloon pops, the knotted stocking will contain the balloon pieces and keep them away from little mouths.) Provide each child with a stocking; then encourage him to throw it in the air and watch it fall to the ground. Or challenge each child to throw his balloon in the air and keep it in the air by gently hitting it upward.

Snowflake Surprise

Use this idea to create a colorful rainbow of snowflakes right inside your classroom. To make one snowflake, write a child's name on the back of a small paper plate. Then tape a six-inch doily to the front of the plate. Place a drop of fingerpaint on the doily; then have a child use her fingers to spread the paint over the doily. Carefully untape the doily and remove it from the plate. Surprise! There's a snowflake print on the plate. To display these frosty creations, punch a hole in the top of each plate. Tie a length of yarn through each hole and then hang the snowflakes in your room.

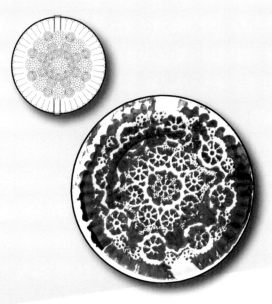

Snowing All Around

Help children drizzle glue over large paper doilies and then cover the doilies with Epsom salts. Hang the doily snowflakes in pairs from your ceiling. Then lead youngsters in reciting the action rhyme shown. It *is* snowing all around!

Way up high

In the winter sky,

Two little snowflakes

Caught my eye.

Down to the ground

They fell without a sound.

And before very long,

It was snowing all around!

Mitten Match

Warm up children's matching skills with mittens! Ask each child to wear a pair of mittens or gloves to school. Have her put one of her mittens into a pile on the floor. Instruct your little ones to form a circle around the mound of mittens. On your signal, invite each child to pick a mitten from the pile and then find its owner.

"Snow-key"–Pokey

Have your little snowfolk form a circle; then get ready for a flurry of movement fun! To modify the verse, name additional pieces of winter attire. Keep warm!

(sung to the tune of "The Hokey-Pokey")

You put your [mittens] in, you put your [mittens] out,
You put your [mittens] in, and you shake them all about.
You do the "Snow-key"–Pokey and you turn yourself around.
That's what it's all about.
"Snow-key"–Pokey!

February Collages

Inspire your toddlers' creative expression by adding tactile materials to your paint center. For example, during the month of February near the easel place a variety of items such as red, white, and pink tissue paper; cellophane wrap; yarn; and doilies. Help each child paint a picture. Then encourage her to press her choice of items into the wet paint to create a collage.

Special Delivery

Encourage your youngsters to spread a little love this Valentine's Day with this easy activity. To prepare, cut hearts in several sizes from red, pink, and white shelf paper (the type that clings but doesn't stick permanently). For each child, peel the backing off a few hearts and stick them onto a sterilized foam tray. Take your little ones on a walk around your school and have them stick hearts on the walls, windows, and doors of other classrooms. The toddlers are here, spreading love and cheer!

Be My Valentine

(sung to the tune of "Clementine")

Won't you be my valentine,
Be my valentine today?
For you are my special friend.
Be my valentine today!

A Smashing Snack

Celebrate Valentine's Day by having youngsters smash up a snack! To make one snack, place a few raspberries inside a resealable plastic bag. If fresh berries are not available, use thawed frozen raspberries. Add one teaspoon of sugar and then seal the bag. Have a child squeeze the berries in the bag until they are completely smashed. Then provide her with a spoon and a heart-shaped piece of toast. Invite her to spoon the mixture out of the bag and spread it on the toast. How tasty!

Santa Pattern

Use with "Santa's Beard Is Soft and White" on page 100.

TEC61237

Read All About It!
Our Class News

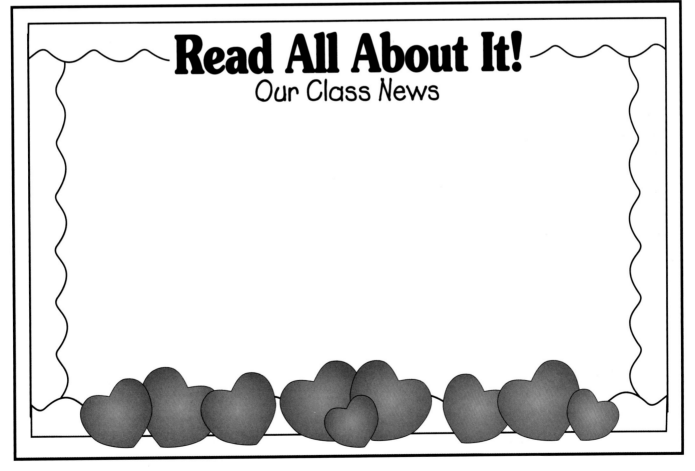

Read All About It!
Our Class News

Note to the teacher: Program a newsletter as desired; then send a copy home with each youngster.

Spectacular Spring

Wind Races

On a really breezy day, take little ones outdoors to feel the power of nature. Give each child a leaf or a feather. Have the children toss their objects up into the air and then watch how the wind carries them along. Which one travels the farthest? Do any escape the wind? Encourage little ones to chase down their windblown treasures before returning to the classroom.

Windblown Puzzles

At this point in the year, your youngsters may be growing bored with your selection of puzzles. So try this twist to spark their interest. To prepare, assemble a puzzle on a sheet of paper (without any frame). Then spread the pieces apart a bit, to make it appear that the pieces have floated away from one another. Trace around each piece in its new position.

Give a child the tracing of the pieces and the puzzle pieces themselves (again, without any frame). Tell her that the spring wind has blown the pieces around and you need her help to reassemble the puzzle. Encourage her to match each piece to its outline. After she accomplishes this task, help her move the pieces back together to assemble the puzzle.

Garden Soup

Take advantage of a warm spring day to conduct this messy-but-fun outdoor experience! Have youngsters put on paint smocks. Head outdoors and have them gather around a few large bowls of water. Explain that you need help making some Garden Soup for the plants and bugs in your play yard. Have them toss in grass, leaves, dirt, twigs, or any other natural materials they find. Provide a few large mixing spoons and make sure everyone gets a turn to stir the earthy concoctions in the bowls! When it seems "just right," pour the Garden Soup onto a natural area or a class garden. Then wash up the bowls, the spoons...and the children!

Snuggle Buddies

Baby animals abound in spring, and toddlers love to hold and cuddle warm, fuzzy critters. So give each child his own Snuggle Buddy to stroke, hug, and baby. For each child, cut a six-inch circle from fake fur. Add pom-pom eyes or use a permanent marker to draw eyes. Invite youngsters to keep their Snuggle Buddies in their cubbies, and you'll be surprised at how often the children will check on their furry companions!

Flower Friends

Flower Friends

Even if it's still cold where you live, you can bring some spring flowers into view with this matching game. Label a sheet of poster board "Flower Friends." Then color and cut out several matching pairs of flowers. For younger children, use the same flower shape and vary the color of each pair. For a more challenging version, vary the flowers' shapes, as well. Glue one of each flower pair to the poster board. If desired, laminate the board and the remaining flower cutouts. Then invite your little ones to match each flower to its "friend" on the board.

Pipe Cleaner Gardens

These crafty flowers look really neat, and they won't ever wilt! To create a pipe cleaner garden, give a child a sheet of corrugated cardboard, such as the side from a packing box. Show her how to stick pipe cleaners into the thin edge of the cardboard, where the holes are visible. Then have her twist and bend the pipe cleaners into spirals and shapes to create a crazy, colorful garden. Mount all the children's gardens side by side on a wall to create a giant garden!

Up Pop the Flowers!

Have your group form a circle—then get growing!

(sung to the tune of "Pop! Goes the Weasel")

We plant some seeds in the dirt.
The rain falls in a shower.
The sun comes out, and what
   do you know?
Up pop the flowers!

Pretend to plant seeds.
Raise arms; then wiggle fingers downward.
Children hold hands and squat.

Release hands. Pop up.

Napkin Know-How

Help youngsters transform pretty spring napkins and recycled containers into lovely vases! Purchase some thin, decorative floral napkins at a local party supply store. Unfold them and cut on the folds so that each piece is a single layer thick. If desired, cut out the floral designs and discard the scraps. Next, help each toddler paint the outside of a clean plastic jar with diluted glue. Then have her place napkin pieces on the jar, overlapping them as she desires. When the jar is completely covered, have the child paint over the pieces with a final coat of glue. Then allow the glue to dry. Ta-da! Beautiful vases for fresh spring flowers!

Pie Plate Symphony

Rumbling spring thunderstorms may make some toddlers uneasy. Help them control their fears by making some rumbling thunder of their very own! Give each child an aluminum pie plate or other disposable baking pan. Then have each youngster roll a piece of aluminum foil into a tight ball. Have each child drop her foil ball into her pan and roll it around to create a thunderous noise. Play some lively music and listen to the symphony begin!

Lovely Ladybugs

Toddlers develop fine-motor skills as they make these one-of-a-kind ladybugs. For each child, glue a small black construction paper circle (head) to a large red construction paper oval (body). Give each child a strip of black adhesive dots (found at office supply stores). Encourage youngsters to peel the dots off the backing and then press them onto the red oval so the dots resemble ladybug spots. If desired, fold the backing to lift the edge of each sticky dot, making it easier for little fingers to grasp and peel it from the paper.

Caterpillar Hop

Little ones get a gross-motor workout when they hop down this curvy caterpillar. On a sidewalk or section of pavement, use chalk to draw a caterpillar with a desired number of connected circular segments. Gather a small group of youngsters. In turn, have each child hop from the end of the caterpillar to its head. To reinforce counting skills, lead waiting toddlers in counting their classmates' hops aloud.

Cool and Yummy for Your Tummy

This St. Patrick's Day activity tastes great! Put a dollop of cold whipped topping into a resealable plastic bag for each child. Add a drop or two of green food coloring; then seal the bag. Invite each child to squish the contents of her bag together to make green fluff. After youngsters see the color mixing and feel the cold temperature of the bag, get another sense involved by inviting each child to taste her bag's contents. Have her open her bag and dip in a cookie or a finger to scoop up a bite of this sweet green treat!

The Tearin' of the Green

Everyone can participate in making this green-as-you've-ever-seen mural for St. Patrick's Day. Give each child a large sheet of green construction paper or green tissue paper. Encourage youngsters to tear the paper to their hearts' content—up, down, or sideways! When the tearing's done, paint some diluted glue onto a large piece of bulletin board paper. Have each child put her pieces on the mural. My goodness, that's *green!*

St. Patrick's Day Squeeze

Use this idea to squeeze out some fine-motor fun with your youngsters! In advance, follow the recipe shown to create a batch of play dough. Next, cover a table with newsprint or a plastic tablecloth. Set the dough at the table along with a jar of green fingerpaint. Invite a child to the area and provide her with a small ball of dough. Direct her to flatten the dough and then drop a spoonful of fingerpaint in the middle of the dough. Have her squeeze and knead the dough until it mixes with the paint and turns green. Allow each child to explore the dough, and then place it in a resealable plastic bag for the child to take home. Play dough and paint—what a great combination!

No-Cook Dough

Ingredients:
4 c. flour
1 c. salt
1³/₄ c. warm water

Teacher preparation:
Combine the flour and salt in a bowl; then add the warm water. Knead the dough for ten minutes. Keep the dough refrigerated in an airtight container until you're ready to use it.

Ring Around the Shamrock

Shimmering shamrocks! Here's the St. Patrick's Day game you've been wishing for! Arrange youngsters in a circle and have them hold hands. Place a large green shamrock shape on the floor in the center of the circle. As a group, circle around the shamrock while singing the song shown. At the end of the song, invite a volunteer to make a wish.

(sung to the tune of "Ring Around the Rosie")

Ring around the shamrock,
Lucky, lucky shamrock,
Shamrock, shamrock,
Let's make a wish!

What's Missing From the Basket?

Twos will enjoy this Easter hunt that builds memory skills. Put two or three different items in an Easter basket. Show each item to the children and say its name several times or even sing it so that your toddlers can remember the name and repeat it. Then ask the children to close their eyes. Remove one item from the basket; then ask the children to open their eyes. Ask them, "What's missing from the basket?" and see if they can name the missing item. Once your toddlers are memory masters with two or three items, try increasing the number.

Take a Peep

Here's an "egg-cellent" way to develop toddlers' memories! Place a different manipulative into each of several different-colored plastic eggs. Invite a child to open each egg and name the object she sees before closing the egg. Then have her try to remember where a particular object is before opening an egg again to check. That's right—the cotton ball *is* in the yellow egg!

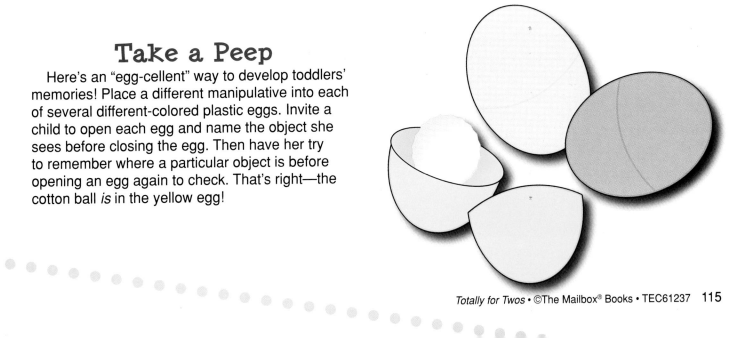

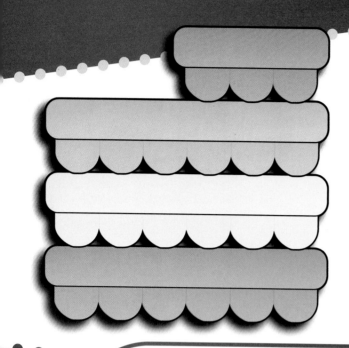

Egg Carton Construction

Before Easter, ask parents to save all their empty foam egg cartons and send them to school after the holiday. After sanitizing the cartons, tape them closed. Now you have wonderful, sturdy building blocks! Cut some cartons into smaller blocks to provide a variety of sizes. Invite youngsters to help you decorate the cartons with paint or stickers, if desired.

Bunny Fun

Dress each of your toddlers in a bunny-ear headband. Then lead your little bunnies in singing the song shown, replacing "hop around" with a different action each time you repeat the song. Hop around, twitch your nose, thump your feet, and shake your tail!

(sung to the tune of "If You're Happy and You know It")

If you like the Easter Bunny, [hop around].
If you like the Easter Bunny, [hop around].
If you like the Easter Bunny,
And you think he's very funny,
If you like the Easter Bunny, [hop around].

Shower Power

The fun will go from a drizzle to a downpour at your water table when you add rainmaking items, such as colanders, strainers, sieves, watering cans, and sifters. If desired, invite visitors to this center to don raincoats and galoshes before reaching in to make it rain. And since the wet fun could get wild, keep some towels on hand as well.

April Showers Bring...Mud!

Invite youngsters to muddle around with these no-mess mud alternatives at your sensory center. Squirt brown liquid paint into several different sizes of resealable plastic bags. Seal the bags; then secure the seals with clear packing tape. Invite youngsters to use their fingers to create designs, shapes, or letters in the mud.

As another mud alternative, provide youngsters with this mushy mud dough for molding, mashing, and making mud pies. To make the mud dough, mix together ½ cup of cold water, one tablespoon of cooking oil, and two tablespoons of brown washable liquid paint. Stir in ½ cup of salt; then add one tablespoon of cornstarch. Gradually add 1½ cups of flour until the dough is soft and smooth. Store the dough in a container; then place it in a center along with plastic spatulas, plastic knives, and different sizes of aluminum tins. (If the dough gets sticky, add flour.) More mud, anyone?

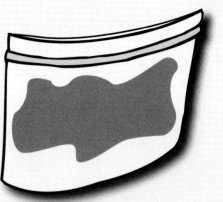

"Spring-y" Singing

After little ones have observed and talked about the changes that take place at this time of year, teach them this song about spring.

(sung to the tune of "Did You Ever See a Lassie?")

Oh, how I love the springtime, the springtime, the springtime!
Oh, how I love the springtime, and I'll tell you why.
I love [all the flowers]; they make me so happy!
Oh, how I love the springtime! Do you love it too?

Continue with the following: *sunny warm days, the warm breezes, animal babies, springtime showers*

Balancing Raindrops

For this movement activity, give each child a raindrop cutout. As you sing the following song, challenge students to hold or balance the raindrops on the named body part. Repeat the song, substituting a different body part each time.

(sung to the tune of "Frère Jacques")

Rain is falling, rain is falling
On my [head], on my [head].
I can feel the raindrop, I can feel the raindrop
On my [head], on my [head].

I Feel...

Talk with youngsters about the harsh and mild weather the spring season typically brings. Then lead little ones in reciting each poem below, comparing the harsh weather to a lion's wild roar and the mild weather to a calm, quiet lamb. At the end of each poem, encourage youngsters to pretend to be the animal described in the poem.

A lion is big
And very strong.
It has a tail
That's very long.
A lion can roar
In a great big way.
I feel like a lion today!

A lamb is small
And soft and sweet.
It has a tail
That's short and neat.
A lamb can bleat
In a quiet way.
I feel like a lamb today!

Read All About It!
Our Class News

Read All About It!
Our Class News

Note to the teacher: Program a newsletter as desired; then send a copy home with each youngster.

Sizzling Summer

Festive Flags

Celebrate Flag Day at your art center with some creative red, white, and blue designs. Place large sheets of white paper at your easel, along with large brushes and red, white, and blue tempera paint. Encourage youngsters to paint their own designs for a patriotic classroom display.

Pop...Pop...Just Can't Stop!

Some toddlers may be frightened of the loud popping sounds made by fireworks. To prepare them to enjoy the exciting sounds, put them in charge of some popping of their own! Give each youngster a square foot of Bubble Wrap cushioning material. Tell the class that you'll count to three, and then each child may stomp on his square, popping as many of the bubbles as he can. Then let the stomping and popping begin! Have everyone stop periodically and look to see how many bubbles they've popped. Youngsters may want to try popping some bubbles with their fingers as well. Your toddlers will get so involved with the fun of popping the bubbles that they won't mind the noise a bit!

pop pop

pop pop

Petite Parade

As Independence Day approaches, plan a patriotic parade right in your own classroom! Use red, white, and blue streamers and other decorations to mark off a parade route that winds around the furniture and through your centers. Invite each of your toddlers to choose a doll or a vehicle to carry as he marches along. Make some star-spangled headbands for your youngsters to wear. Then put on some lively patriotic music and let the marching begin!

Star-Spangled Bottles

Add some patriotic sparkle to your classroom with these star-spangled bottles. To make one star-spangled bottle, remove the label from a clean, clear 16-ounce plastic soda bottle. Pour at least one-half cup of light corn syrup into the bottle. Then add a few drops of food coloring and some star-shaped foil confetti. Hot-glue the lid onto the bottle. Label the bottle with the color of its syrup. Encourage children to comment on the movement of the liquid and stars as they shake, turn, and rotate the bottle.

Watermelon March

Use this idea indoors or outdoors to inspire some melon marching. To prepare an outdoor game, use chalk to draw a number of large watermelon slices in a row on a sidewalk. Alternate drawing one and then two seeds in each slice. Encourage a child to march along the slices stepping only on slices with single seeds.

A Summer Song

Help children think of all the fun things they can do in the summer heat. Then personalize this song for each child, inviting her to fill in her favorite summertime activity in the third line.

(sung to the tune of "You Are My Sunshine")

You know it's summer! Oh, yes, it's summer!
It gets so bright and hot outside.
But [Erin] loves it, 'cause (s)he [goes swimming].
Oh, in summer we have so much fun!

Summer Storytime

With all the fresh fruits available in summer, it's the perfect time to read Eric Carle's *The Very Hungry Caterpillar*. Create a sock puppet to resemble the caterpillar in the story. After reading, have your puppet pretend to eat through some of the foods from your kitchen center. Then invite each child to make a hungry caterpillar puppet of her own. Provide each child with an old, clean sock and a variety of geometric shape stickers. Have her apply the stickers to make eyes, a mouth, and patterned markings for her puppet. Then have youngsters "crawl" their puppets over to your snack table, where they'll find a snack of fresh fruit salad. Look—it's the very hungry toddlers!

Crunchy 'n' Cool

When it's really hot outside, try this idea for a cool treat! Give each child an ice cream stick that is long and narrow. Set out a bowl of wheat germ and have each child roll her ice cream in it. Then head outdoors, find some shade, and invite youngsters to enjoy this cool treat with a crunchy coating.

Ant Detectives

Ants seem to be everywhere in summer, so spend a day focusing on these little critters. Before your toddlers arrive, collect a few ants from your play yard in a clear jar. Invite youngsters to observe them and talk about how they move and climb. Then encourage little ones to make pictures of your insect visitors. Have a child press a fingertip first onto an ink pad (black or red) and then onto paper three times to form the three parts of an ant's body. Have the child use a crayon to add six legs. Keep going and you'll have ants galore! Top off your ant exploration by playing a recording of the classic "The Ants Go Marching" as your youngsters hold their artwork and march around your room in an ant parade!

Summertime Song

Summertime is a fun time! Ask your little ones to name things they like to do in the summer, such as swim, run, build sand castles, and ride tricycles. Then include their ideas in this summertime song.

(sung to the tune of "Mary Had a Little Lamb")

Summer is the time to [play],
Time to [play], time to [play].
Summer is the time to [play].
Enjoy those sunny days!

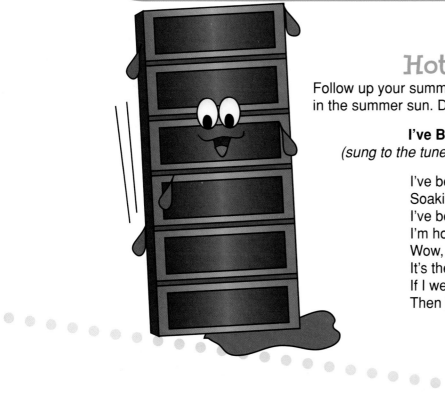

Hot Summer Sun

Follow up your summertime discoveries by singing this little ditty in the summer sun. Don't forget the sunblock!

I've Been Sitting in the Sunshine
(sung to the tune of "I've Been Working on the Railroad")

I've been sitting in the sunshine,
Soaking up the sun.
I've been sitting in the sunshine,
I'm hotter than anyone!
Wow, the sun is really shining,
It's the hottest I've ever felt.
If I were a bar of chocolate,
Then I would surely melt!

A Day at the Beach

Build dramatic-play skills with this gross-motor activity. Lay out a few beach towels on a carpeted area. Then tape a blue crepe paper streamer on the floor about five feet away. Invite a group of youngsters to lounge on the beach towels, but tell them that the water (the blue streamer) is cold! Encourage them, one at a time, to tiptoe to the water and then scurry back to the beach towels. Encourage them to go faster and to not get wet. If desired, add to the experience by spritzing little toes with a spray bottle of water whenever they get close to the water's edge.

Splashing's So Much Fun!

Heading to the pool, lake, or ocean for a swim? Have a splashing good time!

(sung to the tune of "Ten Little Indians")

One big, two big, three big splashes,
Soaking even my eyelashes!
I like making water smashes;
Splashing's so much fun!

Beach Ball Bash

Ask parents to donate beach balls or purchase them on sale. Then encourage pairs of children to toss and roll the balls. Or use the balls to set up an obstacle course for children to run around. You'll have a ball encouraging your children's physical development and social skills!

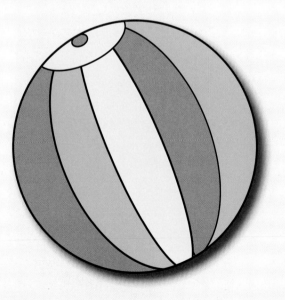

Pool Party

This idea combines scissors and sunshine for a perfect summer-day activity! Set up a child's wading pool outdoors on a sunny day. Add some children's safety scissors and a variety of magazines and catalogs. Invite two or three toddlers (depending on the size of the pool) to sit inside and snip to their heart's content! When the cutting's done, invite the children to keep any pictures they desire and then toss the scraps. Now your pool is ready for more cutting on another day!

Postcard Memory

Use your little ones' vacation memories for a memory-building game. As children go on vacation, ask their parents to bring back postcards from their trips. Have each family bring back two identical postcards. Or—to expedite the process—purchase matching pairs of postcards that show familiar sites in your hometown. Once you have a few pairs of cards, use them to play a memory game. Simply lay out all the cards facedown on the floor and invite one child at a time to try to find a matching pair by turning over two cards. If your toddlers begin to recognize the backs of the cards after several rounds of play, mask the backs with colored Con-Tact paper.

Shapely Swimsuits

Are your little ones excited at the prospect of putting on their swimsuits and splashing in the pool? Have them create some fantastic swimsuits with this art project! Give each child a large paper doll cutout. Then provide glue sticks and a large supply of shapes cut from colorful construction paper. Help each child glue the shapes of her choice onto her paper doll to create a swimsuit. Invite youngsters to further decorate their beach fashions with crayons or markers.

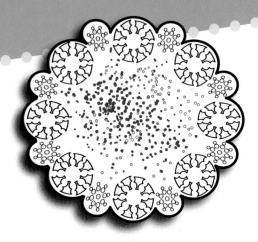

Sandflakes

In the winter there are snowflakes, so in the summer there must be… sandflakes! To make some, cover a table with newspaper. Then give each child in a small group a large paper doily. Help him paint the doily with diluted glue. Then invite him to sprinkle on some plain or colored play sand. Voila! It's a sandflake! When the glue has dried, hang the sandflakes from your ceiling or on a wall to create a summery sandstorm.

Bubbles All Around

Fresh out of bubble solution? Don't fret! Singing this action song to the tune of "Twinkle, Twinkle, Little Star" is the next best thing to catching the real thing.

Bubbles floating all around.	*Pretend to catch bubbles.*
Bubbles fat and bubbles round.	*Make a big circle with arms.*
Bubbles on my toes and nose.	*Point to toes; then point to nose.*
Blow a bubble...up it goes!	*Pretend to blow a bubble; then point up.*
Bubbles floating all around.	*Pretend to catch bubbles.*
Bubbles falling to the ground.	*Sing slowly and sink to the ground.*

Bubble Potion

⅛ c. dishwashing liquid
1 c. water

This simple solution and the bubble-blowing tools suggested below are all you'll need to burst into bubble-blowing mania. Consider mixing a personalized plastic container full of the solution for each child. Or create a laboratory for the serious study of bubbles by multiplying the soap and water amounts as needed to fill a water table full of the solution. Place the water table outside along with these bubble-blowing tools made from inexpensive and easy-to-find household items. Students are sure to be delighted to discover that they can create billions of bubbles!

Wand suggestions:
• Twist a pipe cleaner as shown. Dip the loop into the bubble solution and blow through the opening or wave the wand in the air.
• Dip a plastic fly swatter into the bubble solution; then wave it through the air.
• Tape a set of plastic soda-can rings to one end of a dowel. Dip the rings in the bubble solution; then wave them through the air.

The Flower and the Bee

In summertime bees and flowers are best friends. Give each child a small bee stick puppet and a flower stick puppet. Don't forget to make a set for yourself! Then lead little ones in reciting the poem and performing the actions shown.

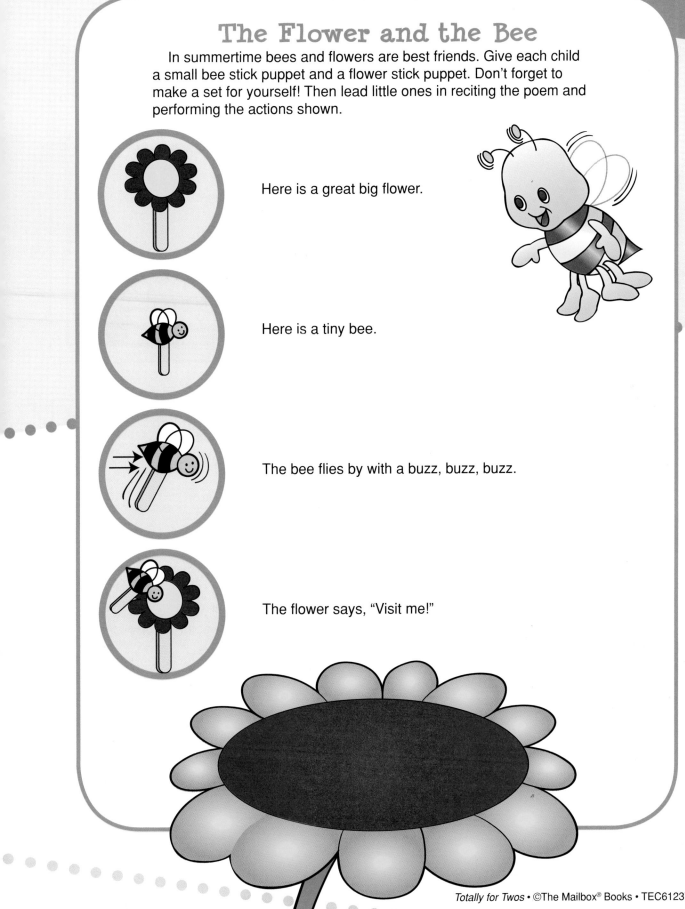

Here is a great big flower.

Here is a tiny bee.

The bee flies by with a buzz, buzz, buzz.

The flower says, "Visit me!"

Read All About It!
Our Class News

Totally for Twos • ©The Mailbox® Books • TEC61237

Read All About It!
Our Class News

Totally for Twos • ©The Mailbox® Books • TEC61237

Note to the teacher: Program a newsletter as desired; then send a copy home with each youngster.